Visit us at

www.syngress.com

Syngress is committed to publishing high-quality books for IT Professionals and delivering those books in media and formats that fit the demands of our customers. We are also committed to extending the utility of the book you purchase via additional materials available from our Web site.

SOLUTIONS WEB SITE

To register your book, visit www.syngress.com/solutions. Once registered, you can access our solutions@syngress.com Web pages. There you may find an assortment of valueadded features such as free e-books related to the topic of this book, URLs of related Web sites, FAQs from the book, corrections, and any updates from the author(s).

ULTIMATE CDs

Our Ultimate CD product line offers our readers budget-conscious compilations of some of our best-selling backlist titles in Adobe PDF form. These CDs are the perfect way to extend your reference library on key topics pertaining to your area of expertise, including Cisco Engineering, Microsoft Windows System Administration, CyberCrime Investigation, Open Source Security, and Firewall Configuration, to name a few.

DOWNLOADABLE E-BOOKS

For readers who can't wait for hard copy, we offer most of our titles in downloadable Adobe PDF form. These e-books are often available weeks before hard copies, and are priced affordably.

SYNGRESS OUTLET

Our outlet store at syngress.com features overstocked, out-of-print, or slightly hurt books at significant savings.

SITE LICENSING

Syngress has a well-established program for site licensing our e-books onto servers in corporations, educational institutions, and large organizations. Contact us at sales@syngress.com for more information.

CUSTOM PUBLISHING

Many organizations welcome the ability to combine parts of multiple Syngress books, as well as their own content, into a single volume for their own internal use. Contact us at sales@syngress.com for more information.

SYNGRESS®

No Tech Hacking:
A Guide to Social Engineering, Dumpster Diving, and Shoulder Surfing

Johnny Long

Scott Pinzon, CISSP, Technical Editor
Jack Wiles, Contributor
Kevin D. Mitnick, Foreword Contributor

KEY	SERIAL NUMBER
001	HJIRTCV764
002	PO9873D5FG
003	829KM8NJH2
004	BAL923457U
005	CVPLQ6WQ23
006	VBP965T5T5
007	HJJJ863WD3E
008	2987GVTWMK
009	629MP5SDJT
010	IMWQ295T6T

PUBLISHED BY
Syngress Publishing, Inc.
Elsevier, Inc.
30 Corporate Drive
Burlington, MA 01803

No Tech Hacking: A Guide to Social Engineering, Dumpster Diving, and Shoulder Surfing

Printed in the United States of America
1 2 3 4 5 6 7 8 9 0

ISBN 13: 978-1-59749-215-7

Publisher: Andrew Williams
Technical Editor: Scott Pinzon
Page Layout and Art: SPi

For information on rights, translations, and bulk sales, contact Matt Pedersen, Commercial Sales Director and Rights, at Syngress Publishing; email m.pedersen@elsevier.com.

Johnny Long, Author

What's the story with the proceeds?

It's simple, really. My proceeds from this book are going to AOET (aoet.org), an organization that provides food, education and medical care to children left in the wake of Africa's HIV/AIDS epidemic. More than an aid organization, AOET aims to disrupt the cycle of poverty and hopelessness in sub-Saharan Africa through empowerment programs and job training, enabling children and adults to be self-sustaining, restoring not only their health but their pride and hope for a brighter future. A single book purchase made through my Amazon associates account (linked from any of my websites, or though http://tiniuri.com/f/Xpc) will generate enough income for AOET to feed a child for an entire month. Other retail purchases (which generate half as much income) will provide either medical services or educational supplies and funding for a single child through a donation pool set aside for those purposes. Because I am called to "look after orphans and widows in their distress" (James 1:27), and I know from personal experience how mutually transformative it can be to take that calling seriously. Hamlet was onto something when he wondered, "Whether this nobler in the mind to suffer the slings and arrows of outrageous fortune or to take arms against a sea of troubles, and by opposing, end them."

"I'm Johnny. I Hack Stuff."

There are many people to thank this time around, and I won't get to them all. But I'll give it my best shot. First and foremost, thanks to God for the many blessings in my life. Christ for the Living example, and the Spirit of God that encourages me to live each day with real purpose. This book is more a "God thing" than a "Johnny thing." Thanks to my wife and four wonderful kids. Words can't express how much you mean to me. Thanks for putting up with the real me.

I'd like to thank the members of the Shmoo group for fielding lots of questions, and to my book team: Alex, CP, Deviant, Eric, Freshman, Garland, Jack, Joshua, Marc, Ross, Russ, Vince and Yoshi. It was great to have your support, especially in such a tight timeframe. Thanks also to Scott Pinzon, for being a mentor and a great editor.

You've taught me so much. I'd also like to thank Vince Ritts for taking the time to plant no-tech hacking seed all those years ago.

And to the many friends and fans that have supported my work over the years, a final thanks. You make it very difficult to remain anti-social.

Be sure to check out our companion website at http://notechhacking.com as we continue the story of the no-tech hacker.

Johnny Long is a Christian by grace, a professional hacker by trade, a pirate by blood, a ninja in training, a security researcher and author. He can be found lurking at his website (http://johnny.ihackstuff.com). He is the founder of Hackers For Charity (http://ihackcharities.org), an organization that provides hackers with job experience while leveraging their skills for charities that need those skills.

Technical Editor

Scott Pinzon, CISSP, is Editor-in-Chief for LiveSecurity, a service offered by Watch-Guard Technologies in Seattle. Pinzon has edited, written, and/or published well over 1,500 security alerts and "best practices" articles to LiveSecurity subscribers, who have tripled in number during his tenure. Pinzon has worked in the fields of security, encryption products, e-commerce, and voice messaging, with 18 years of experience writing about high-tech products for clients both large (Weyerhaeuser IT) and small (Seattle's first cash machine network). LiveSecurity training videos that Pinzon has co-written and directed have accumulated more than 100,000 views on Google Video and YouTube. He also hosts the internationally respected podcast, Radio Free Security. Pinzon was story editor for *Stealing the Network: How to Own a Shadow*, available from Syngress. He still believes he made the right call when he turned down the publisher who asked him to ghost-write books for Mr. T.

Contributing Author

Jack Wiles is a security professional with over 30 years' experience in security-related fields, including computer security, disaster recovery, and physical security. He is a professional speaker and has trained federal agents, corporate attorneys, and internal auditors on a number of computer crime-related topics. He is a pioneer in presenting on a number of subjects that are now being labeled "Homeland Security" topics. Well over 10,000 people have attended one or more of his presentations since 1988. Jack is also a cofounder and president of TheTrainingCo. He is in frequent contact with members of many state and local law enforcement agencies as well as special agents with the U.S. Secret Service, FBI, U.S. Customs, Department of Justice, the Department of Defense, and numerous members of high-tech crime units. He was also appointed as the first president of the North Carolina InfraGard chapter, which is now one of the largest chapters in the country. He is also a founding member and "official" MC of the U.S. Secret Service South Carolina Electronic Crimes Task Force.

Jack is also a Vietnam veteran who served with the 101st Airborne Division in Vietnam in 1967–68. He recently retired from the U.S. Army Reserves as a lieutenant colonel and was assigned directly to the Pentagon for the final seven years of his career. In his spare time, he has been a senior contributing editor for several local, national, and international magazines.

Foreword Contributor

With more than fifteen years of experience in exploring computer security, **Kevin Mitnick** is a largely self-taught expert in exposing the vulnerabilities of complex operating systems and telecommunications devices. His hobby as an adolescent consisted of studying methods, tactics, and strategies used to circumvent computer security, and to learn more about how computer systems and telecommunication systems work.

In building this body of knowledge, Kevin gained unauthorized access to computer systems at some of the largest corporations on the planet and penetrated some of the most resilient computer systems ever developed. He has used both technical and non-technical means to obtain the source code to various operating systems and telecommunications devices to study their vulnerabilities and their inner workings.

As the world's most famous hacker, Kevin has been the subject of countless news and magazine articles published throughout the world. He has made guest appearances on numerous television and radio programs, offering expert commentary on issues related to information security. In addition to appearing on local network news programs, he has made appearances on 60 Minutes, The Learning Channel, Tech TV's Screen Savers, Court TV, Good Morning America, CNN's Burden of Proof, Street Sweep, and Talkback Live, National Public Radio, and as a guest star on ABC's new spy drama "Alias". Mitnick has served as a keynote speaker at numerous industry events, hosted a weekly talk radio show on KFI AM 640 in Los Angeles, testified before the United States Senate, written for Harvard Business Review and spoken for Harvard Law School. His first best-selling book, *The Art of Deception*, was published in October 2002 by Wiley and Sons Publishers. His second title, *The Art of Intrusion*, was released in February 2005.

Special Contributors

Alex Bayly approaches perfectly normal situations as though he were prepping a social engineering gig, much to the irritation of his wife. This habit has resulted in a rather large collection of pointless and frankly useless discarded ID cards for people he doesn't even know. He currently is employed as a senior security consultant in the UK, conducting social engineering work and traditional penetration testing.

CP is an active member of DC949, and co-organizer of Open CTF, the annual Open hacking contest at DefCon. Working officially as a software architect, his true passion lies in information security. He has developed several open source security tools, and continues his work on browser based security. Currently, CP is working on expanding oCTF, and opening human knowledge as a whole.

Matt Fiddler leads a Threat Management Team for a large Fortune 100 Company. Mr. Fiddler's research into lock bypass techniques has resulted in several public disclosures of critical lock design flaws. Mr. Fiddler began his career as an Intelligence Analyst with the United States Marine Corps. Since joining the commercial sector in 1992, he has spent the last 15 years enhancing his extensive expertise in the area of UNIX and Network Engineering, Security Consulting, and Intrusion Analysis.

When he's not dragging his knuckles as a defcon goon or living the rock-star lifestyle of a shmoo, **freshman** is the clue-by-4 and acting President of The Hacker Foundation. His involvement in the security/Information Assurance realm has been a long treacherous road filled with lions, tigers, and careless red teams. When he's not consulting, he can be found getting into heated discussions regarding operational security, Information Assurance best practice, and trusted computing over a bottle of good scotch.

Russell Handorf currently works for a prominent stock exchange as their senior security analyst and also serves on the board of directors for the FBI's

Philadelphia InfraGard Chapter. Prior to this, Mr. Handorf consulted for the US federal and state and local governments, law enforcement, companies and educational institutions where he performed training, security audits and assessments. His industry experience started as the CIO and director of research and development for a Philadelphia based wireless broadband solutions provider.

Ross Kinard is currently a senior a Lafayette High School. Ross works doing cleaning, god-awful cooking, and labor dog services. A constant interest in bad ideas and all types of physical security has kept him entertained with projects from pneumatic cannons to lockpicking.

Eric Michaud is currently a Computer and Physical Security Analyst for the Vulnerability Assessment Team at Argonne National Laboratory. A co-founder of The Open Organisation Of Lockpickers (TOOOL) – US Division and is actively involved in security research for hardware and computer security. When not attending and collaborating with fellow denizens at security events locally and international he may be found residing in the Mid-West. Though classically trained as an autodidact he received his B.S. from Ramapo College of New Jersey.

While paying the bills as a network engineer and security consultant, **Deviant Ollam**'s first and strongest love has always been teaching. A graduate of the New Jersey Institute of Technology's "Science, Technology, & Society" program, he is fascinated by the interplay between human values and developments in the technical world. A fanatical supporter of the philosophy that the best way to increase security is to publicly disclose vulnerabilities, Deviant has given lockpicking presentations at universities, conferences, and even the United States Military Academy at West Point.

Marc Weber Tobias, Esq. is an Investigative Attorney and physical security specialist in the United States. He has written five law enforcement textbooks dealing with criminal law, security, and communications. Marc was employed for several years by the Office of Attorney General, State of South Dakota, as the Chief of the Organized Crime Unit. Mr. Tobias has lectured throughout the world to law enforcement agencies and consulted with clients and lock manufacturers in many countries. His law firm handles internal affairs investigations for certain government agencies, as well as civil investigations for private clients. Mr. Tobias is also employed by both private and public clients to analyze high security locks and security systems for bypass capability and has been involved in the design of security hardware to prevent bypass. Marc Tobias, through www.security.org, has issued many security alerts regarding product defects in security hardware. Mr. Tobias authored *Locks, Safes, and Security*, the primary reference for law enforcement agencies throughout the world, and the companion, LSS+, the multimedia edition.

Contents

Foreword

Annually, I attend a number of security conferences around the world. One speaker that I never miss is Johnny Long. Not only is Johnny one of the most entertaining speakers on the security circuit, his presentations are filled with interesting ideas that are corner stoned in what should be the first defense in security mitigation. Common sense.

Not only does Johnny challenge you not to ignore the obvious and to be more aware of your surroundings, his no tech hacking takes on a MacGyver approach to bypassing expensive security technology that sometimes are wholly relied upon to secure data and the premises.

Every day, corporations spend thousands of dollars on high-tech security defenses, but fail to give attention to the simple bypasses that no-tech hackers can leverage to their benefit. In this book Johnny presents eye-opening exploits that security professionals must take into consideration. In their haste to complete tasks and move along to the next topic, many security managers are overlooking simple flaws that render their high-dollar technologies, useless.

It is this complacency by security departments to ignore the simple threats; attackers are given the upper hand during a compromise. An intruder will always pursue the path of least resistance in an attack, while many businesses plan for the Mission Impossible scenario. Johnny will surprise you by bypassing a physical lock with a hand towel, tailgating behind a group of employees to enter a building, digging in the trash to uncover sensitive proprietary information, using Google and P2P networks to dig up sensitive information posted by internal employees and consumers alike, and then showing you how all of these things pooled together may provide the open door for an attacker to exploit you.

The most overlooked factor in securing a business is the people factor. The most expensive technologies will provide you no benefit if an attacker can call up an employee and convince them to turn it off or alter its setting to create a window of opportunity. Social engineering is perhaps the hacker's favorite weapon of choice. Why waste time on an elaborate technical compromise, when you can make a few phone calls to gather seemingly innocuous information from unsuspecting people and leverage them into opening the door?

In my past life as a black-hat hacker, social engineering enabled me to get my foot in the door in record time—minutes. Afterwards, I would have to find and exploit technical flaws to achieve my objectives. The example of social engineering that Jack Wiles provided in this book may appear to be too good to be true. It isn't. And that's just a single pretext—the human imagination could think of many, many more. The question is, would you or your co-workers, employers, or mom and dad fall for it? The chapter on social engineering will offer insight on how no-tech hackers manipulate their victims into what is probably the most common method of attack for which no technological solution will safeguard your information.

Both consumers and businesses will find valuable information that creates awareness, within the pages of Johnny's *No-Tech Hacking*. This book clearly illustrates the often-ignored threats that IT managers should take into consideration when designing security plans to protect their business. Not only will business find the content of this book riveting, consumers will also garner knowledge on methods to protect themselves from identity theft, burglary, and hardening their defenses on home systems maintained by a computer. Much like his *Google Hacking*, Johnny has once again offered an entertaining but thought-provoking look into hacking techniques and the ingenuity being utilized by your adversaries.

—*Kevin Mitnick*

Introduction

What Is "No-Tech Hacking?"

When I got into this field, I knew I would have to stay ahead of the tech curve. I spent many sleepless nights worming through my home network trying to learn the ropes. My practice paid off. After years of hard work and dedicated study, I founded a small but elite pen testing team. I was good, my *foo* strong. Networks fell prostrate before me. My co-workers looked up to me, and I thought I was The Man. Then I met Vince.

In his mid-40s, hawk-eyed, and vaguely European looking, Vince blended in with the corporate crowd; he was most often seen in a black leather trench coat, a nice dress shirt, dark slacks, black wing tips and the occasional black fedora. He had a definite aura. Tales of his exploits were legendary. Some said he had been a fed, working deep-black projects for the government. Other insisted he was some kind of mercenary genius, selling his dark secrets to the highest bidder.

He was brilliant. He could do interesting and seemingly impossible things. He could pick locks, short-circuit electronic systems, and pluck information out of the air with fancy electronic gear. He once showed me a system he built called a "van Eck" something-or-other.[1] It could sniff the electromagnetic radiation coming from a CRT and reassemble it, allowing him to eavesdrop on someone's computer monitor from a quarter mile away. He taught me that a black-and-white TV could be used to monitor

---

[1] http://en.wikipedia.org/wiki/Van_Eck_phreaking

900MHz cellular phone conversations. I still remember hunching over a table in my basement going at the UHF tuner post of an old black-and-white TV with a pair of needle-nosed pliers. When I heard a cellular phone conversation coming through that old TV's speaker, I decided then and there I would learn everything I could from Vince.

I was incredibly intimidated before our first gig. Fortunately, we had different roles. I was to perform an internal assessment, which emulated an insider threat. If an employee went rogue, he could do unspeakable damage to a network. In order to properly emulate this, our clients provided us a workspace, a network jack, and the username and password of a legitimate, non-administrative user. I was tasked with leveraging those credentials to gain administrative control of critical network systems. If I gained access to confidential records stored within a corporate database, for example, my efforts were considered successful. I had a near-perfect record with internal assessments and was confident in my abilities.

Vince was to perform a physical assessment that emulated an external physical threat. The facility had top-notch physical security. They had poured a ton of money into expensive locks, sensors, and surveillance gear. I knew Vince would obliterate them all with his high-tech superpowers. The gig looked to be a real slam-dunk with him working the physical and me working the internal. We were the "dream team" of security geeks.

When Vince insisted I help him with the physical part of the assessment, I just about fell over. I imagined a James Bond movie, with Vince as "Q" and myself (of course) as James Bond in ninja assault gear. Vince would supply the gadgets, like the van Eck thingamabob and I would infiltrate the perimeter and spy on their surveillance monitors or something. I giggled to myself about the unnatural things we would do to the electronic keypad systems or the proximity locks. I imagined the looks on the guard's faces when we duct-taped them to their chairs after silently rappelling down from the ceiling of the surveillance room.

I couldn't wait to get started. I told Vince to hand over the alien gadgets we would use to pop the security. When he told me he hadn't brought any gadgets, I laughed and poked him. I never knew Vince was a kidder. When he told me he really didn't bring any gear, I briefly considered pushing him over, but I had heard he was a black belt in like six different martial arts, so I just politely asked him what the heck he was thinking. He said we were going to be creative. The mercenary genius, the storm center of all the swirling rumors, hadn't brought any gear. I asked him how creative a person could be when attacking a highly secured building without any gear. He just looked at me and gave me this goofy grin. I'll never forget that grin.

We spent the morning checking out the site. It consisted of several multistory buildings and a few employee parking lots, all enclosed by protective fencing. Everyone came and went through a front gate. Fortunately, the gate was open and unguarded. With Vince driving, we rounded one building and parked behind it, in view of the loading docks.

"There," he said.

"Where?" I asked.

"There," he repeated.

Vince's sense of humor sucked sometimes. I could never quite tell when he was giving me crap. I followed the finger and saw a loading dock. Just past the bay doors, several workers carried packages around. "The loading dock?" I asked.

"That's your way in."

I made a "Pffft" sound.

"Exactly. Easy." he said.

"I didn't mean 'Pffft' as in *easy*. I meant 'Pffft' as in *there's people there* and you said *I* was going in."

"There are, and you are," he said. Vince was helpful that way. "Just look like you belong. Say hello to the employees. Be friendly. Comment on the weather."

I did, and I did. Then I did, and I did and I found myself inside. I walked around, picked up some blueprints of tanks and military-looking stuff, photocopied them and left. Just like that. I'm skipping the description of my heart pounding at 400 beats per minute and the thoughts of what military prison would be like and whether or not the rumors about Bubba were true, but I did it. And it was an incredible rush. It was social engineering at its simplest, and it worked wonders. No one questioned me. I suppose it was just too awkward for them. I couldn't hide my grin as I walked to the car. Vince was nowhere to be found. He emerged from the building a few minutes later, carrying a small stack of letter-sized paper.

"How did you get in?" I asked.

"Same way you did."

"So why didn't you just do it yourself?" I asked.

"I had to make sure it would work first."

I was Vince's guinea pig but it didn't really matter. I was thrilled and ready for more. The next building we targeted looked like an absolute fortress. There were no loading docks and the only visible entrance was the front door. It was wood and steel—too much like a castle door for my taste—and approximately six inches thick, sporting a proximity card-reader device. We watched as employees swiped a badge, pulled open the doors and walked in. I suggested we tailgate. I was on a roll. Vince shook his head. He obviously had other plans. He walked towards the building and slowed as we approached the front door. Six feet from the door, he stopped. I walked a step past him and turned around, my back to the door.

"Nice weather," he said, looking past me at the door.

"Ehrmm, yeah," I managed.

"Good day for rock climbing."

I began to turn around to look at the building. I hadn't considered climbing it.

"No," he said. "Don't turn around. Let's chat."

"Chat?" I asked. "About what?"

"You see that Bears game last night?" he asked. I had no clue what he was talking about or even who the Bears were but he continued. "Man, that was something else. The way that team works together, it's almost as if…" Vince stopped in mid-sentence as the front door opened. An employee pushed the door open, and headed towards the parking lot. "They move as a single unit," he continued. I couldn't help myself. I turned around. The door had already closed.

"Crap," I said. "We could have made it inside."

"Yes, a coat hanger."

Vince said strange stuff sometimes. That was just part of the package. It wasn't crazy-person stuff, it was just stuff that most people were too dense to understand. I had a pretty good idea I had just witnessed his first crazy-person moment. "Let's go," he said. "I need a washcloth. I need to go back to the hotel." I had no idea why he needed a washcloth, but I was relieved to hear he was still a safe crazy person. I had heard of axe murderers, but never washcloth murderers.

We passed the ride back to the hotel in silence; Vince seemed lost in his thoughts. He pulled up in front of the hotel, parked, and told me to wait for him. He emerged a few minutes later with a wire coat hanger and a damp washcloth. He tossed them into the back seat. "This should work," he said, sliding into his seat and closing the doors. I was afraid to ask. Pulling away from the hotel, he continued. "I should be able to get in with these."

I gave him a look. I can't exactly say what the look was, but I imagine it was somewhere between "I've had an unpleasant olfactory encounter" and "There's a tarantula on your head." Either way, I was pretty convinced he'd lost his mind or had it stolen by aliens. I pretended not to hear him. He continued anyhow.

"Every building has to have exits," he said. "Federal law dictates that in the case of an emergency, exit doors must operate from the inside out without the user having any prior knowledge of its operation." I blinked and looked up at the sky through the windshield. I wondered if the aliens were coming for me next. "Furthermore, the exit must not require the use of any key or special token. Exit doors are therefore very easy to get out of."

"This has something to do with that door we were looking at, doesn't it?" I asked. The words surprised me. Vince and I were close to the same operating frequency.

He looked at me, and then I knew what *my look* looked like. I instinctively swatted at the tarantula that I could practically feel on my head. "This has *everything* to do with that door," he said, looking out the front window and hanging a left. We were headed back to the site. "The front door of that facility," he continued, "is formidable. It uses a very heavy-duty magnetic bolting system. My guess is that it would resist the impact of a 40-mile-an-hour vehicle. The doors are very thick, probably shielded, and the prox system is expensive."

"But you have a washcloth," I said. I couldn't resist.

"Exactly. Did you notice the exit mechanism on the door?"

I hadn't, and bluffing was out of the question. "No," I admitted.

"You need to notice *everything*," he said, pausing to glare at me. I nodded and he continued. "The exit mechanism is a silver-colored metal bar about waist-high."

I took my shot. "Oh, right. A push bar." The term sounded technical enough.

"No, not a push bar." Access denied. "The bar on that door is touch-sensitive. It doesn't operate by pressure; it operates when it senses it has been touched. Very handy in a fire." We pulled through the site's gate and parked. Vince unbuckled and grabbed the hanger and the washcloth from the back seat. He had untwisted the hanger, creating one long straight piece of strong, thin wire. He folded it in half, laid the washcloth on one end and folded the end of the hanger around it, then bent the whole thing to form a funny 90-degree-angled white washcloth flag. I smartly avoided any comment about using it to surrender to the guards. "Let's go," he said.

We walked to the front door. It was nearly 6:00 P.M. and very few employees were around. He walked up to the door, jammed the washcloth end of the hangar between the doors at waist height and started twisting the hanger around. I could hear the washcloth flopping around on the other side of the door. Within seconds, I heard a muffled *cla-chunk* and Vince pulled the door open and walked inside. I stood there gawking at the door as it closed behind him. The door reopened, and Vince stuck his head out. "You coming?"

The customer brief was a thing to behold. After the millions of dollars they had spent to secure that building, they learned that the entire system had been defeated with a washcloth and a wire coat hanger, all for want of a $50 gap plate for the door. The executives were incredulous and demanded proof, which Vince provided in the form of a field trip. I never learned what happened as a result of that demonstration, but I will never forget the lesson I learned: the simplest solutions are often the most practical.

Sure we could have messed with the prox system, figured out the magnetic tolerances on the lock or scaled the walls and used our welding torches—just like in the movies—to cut a hole in the ceiling, but we didn't have to. This is the essence of no-tech hacking. It requires technical knowledge to reap the full benefit of a no-tech attack, but technical knowledge is not required to repeat it. Worst of all, despite the simplicity, a no-tech attack is perhaps the most deadly and misunderstood.

Through the years, I've learned to follow Vince's advice. I now notice *everything* and I try to keep complicated thinking reigned in. Now, I'm hardly ever off duty. I constantly see new attack vectors, the most dangerous of which can be executed by anyone possessing the will to do so.

The Key to No-Tech Hacking

The key to no-tech hacking is to think simply, be aware, and to travel eyes open, head up. For example, when I go to a mall or some other socially dense atmosphere, I watch people. To me, strangers are an interesting puzzle and I reflexively try to figure out as much about them as I can. When I pass a businessman in an airport, my mind goes into overdrive as I try to sense his seat number and social status; make out his medical problems; fathom his family situation (or sense his sexual orientation); figure out his financial standing; infer his income level; deduce his dietary habits; and have a guess at his home address. When I go to a restaurant, I drift in and out of conversations around me, siphoning interesting tidbits of information. My attention wanders as I analyze my surroundings, taking it all in. When I walk through the parking lot of a building, I check out the vehicles along the way to determine what goes on inside and who the building's residents might be. I do all this stuff not because of my undiagnosed attention deficit disorder but because it's become a habit as a result of my job. I have personally witnessed the power of perception. When faced with tough security challenges, I don't charge. I hang back and I watch. A good dose of heightened perception levels the playing field every time.

—*Johnny Long*

Chapter 1

Dumpster Diving

Hackers pilfer secret data in lots of different ways, but did you they can suck sensitive data right off a corporate network without even touching the network? You might think I'm talking about wireless technology, which doesn't require any "touching" at all, but I'm not. Be a good sport and don't read the two "D" words written in big bold letters at the top of this page, and act surprised when I tell you hackers can accomplish this without relying on a single bit of technology (punny). Or, don't play along, and pretend not to be surprised. In fact, maybe it's better you go on thinking your personal or corporate secrets aren't sitting exposed in a dumpster somewhere, waiting for a no-tech hacker to snatch them up. In that case you better just skip this chapter.

Introduction to Dumpster Diving

Dumpster diving involves… *diving* into *dumpsters* in search of valuable information. I know, it's bad form to use the phrase in the definition of the phrase, but that's what dumpster diving is, or what it *used* to be. These days, diving is optional. As this next photo shows, I find interesting stuff just hanging out in the open, waiting to be grabbed.

I find valuable trash in plain view all the time, like the insurance bill shown in the next photo, which is visible through the clear trash liner.

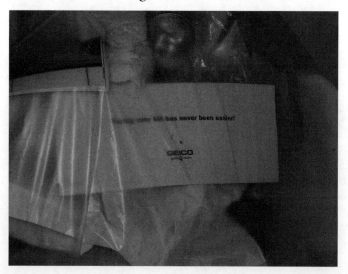

The next photo shows a pile of discarded documents belonging to a network administrator. I used my strong power of intuition to determine that these belonged to an administrator.

Judging from the next photo, "Fred" is obviously unhappy with his job—he's hard at work surfing careerbuilder.com in search of a new position. This printout reveals an awful lot about Fred. What else can you tell me about him based on this single document?

For starters, it's very probable that Fred's got a four-year degree of some kind, otherwise he wouldn't have printed out a job description that required that much schooling. It's a good bet that he makes a good deal less than $80,000 a year, judging from the position's salary, that he's looking for a full-time gig, and that he's probably working in the Defense Aerospace industry. Stuff like this makes me want to write Foreign Intelligence Service Recruiting for Dummies. Forget all the hard work of finding a mark's name, email address, employer, educational background, department of defense affiliation and career aspirations. All it takes is a brainless dumpster sweep to find juicy recruiting targets.

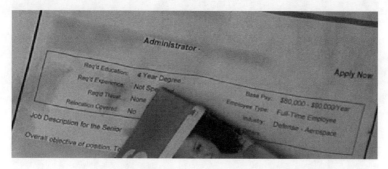

Personal info is one thing, but I find sensitive corporate information all the time as well. The next photo shows a purchase order, detailing a company's several thousand-dollar purchase.

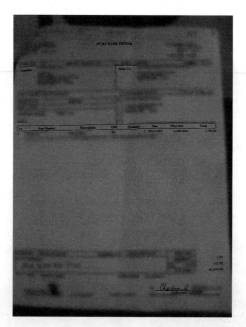

Although the form is quite dated, it lists a great deal of information including the client's name, address and phone number, a description of the service (which is technical in nature and reveals information about the inner workings of the client), and authorized management signatures (which may be of use to a forger if the manager is still employed with the service company).

A purchase order isn't really a big deal, but I think the next document might be. It's marked "Do Not Disseminate."

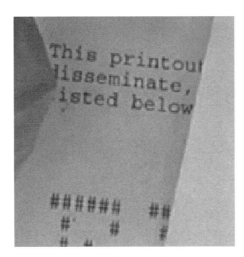

Disseminate is such a big word that I think people might not understand what it means. This causes obvious problems when it comes time to discard (or should I say *throw away*) the document. Confusing phrases abound though, like *proprietary information*. I found it written on the next document which was lying on the ground outside a dumpster.

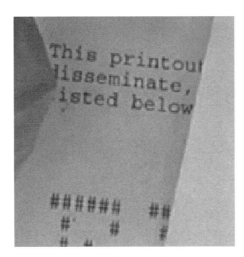

A clearer phrase to use might be "For Internal Use Only." But even this phrase is obviously somewhat confusing, because I found it written on this now-famous dumpster dangling document.

I guess I miss the point of warning phrases like these. Inigo Montoya had it right in The Princess Bride when he said "You keep using that [phrase]. I do not think it means what you think it means." I vote for banning confusing phrases like Proprietary Information and Do not disseminate. I vote for splashing every document with a clearer tagline like "Put In Parking Lot For Everyone To Read." At least then there's no confusion about what people are supposed to do when it comes time to throw the thing away.

And just in case you think it's an awful lot of effort to walk past a dumpster and grab stuff that's hanging out of it, I've got good news. Sometimes if you're really lucky, all you have to do is stand in a parking lot on a windy day and wait for sensitive stuff to blow right into your face. That's exactly what happened to my buddy Mike at work one day. He grabbed the offending document and after discovering it didn't belong to his employer, he shared it with me. Now I'm sharing it with you.

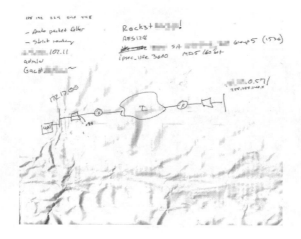

This bunch of scribble might not look like much to the untrained eye, but any techie will tell you that this map outlines everything needed to take control of a computer network. The (blurred) IP addresses is a real live address, and the username (admin) and password (blurred, beginning with the letters "G" and "a") provide everything needed to log into the machine as an administrator. Another password (blurred, beginning with "R0ck3t") written at the top of the page provides access to another private IP address (blurred, ending with "0.57"), and perhaps to other machines on the private network. The routing and subnet map along with terms like packet filter and strict routing reveal that the scribbler is technically adept, while terms like AES128, MD5 and ipsec indicate that he or she is at least somewhat security-conscious, but the simple fact remains that this document was tossed aside (along with other documents Mike didn't bother to pluck out of the air) as if it were not important.

A high-tech attacker could spend hours, days, or weeks poking at the external box in an attempt to bypass AES-128 encryption and IPSEC to gain access to the private network behind it. Even then, he or she would struggle to bypass the security of the internal machines, to gain access to the "rocket" box. On the other hand, a no-tech hacker can bypass the security of the entire network in moments, just by peeling a document off his face and hanging on to it.

Fortunately, this kind of parking lot fodder is pretty rare. Admittedly, I've only seen a handful of cases that were this blatant. Most of the time I have to really push the limits and actually stick my head into the dumpster and peer inside. I discovered the next document in a dumpster on top of an open box of similar papers. The doc lists client names, account information, and a handy list of sales reps, the commissions they made and their Social Security numbers. A rival company might be interested in these documents, but an identity thief would have a field day with them.

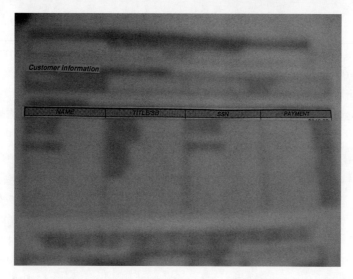

Customer Information

When I found the dumpster shown in the next photo, I was disappointed because it had obviously just been emptied. The scattering of white envelopes left behind seemed innocuous enough, until I read the words *healthcare information* in bold red lettering. The rough, ripped edge of the envelope shown in the next photo seemed to suggest that some dummy had gotten the invoice in the mail, opened it, stuffed it back in the envelope and threw it out for a creepy (talented) no-tech hacker like me. If this were my invoice, I would have shredded it, then used the scraps to line my cat's litter box—which seems to deter even the most dedicated of dumpster divers.

But the white envelope was not alone in this dumpster. I spotted a few more envelopes, each bearing the same scarlet lettering, and realized that each of the other envelopes (like the one shown in the next photo) was *unopened*, and each one had a different mailing address.

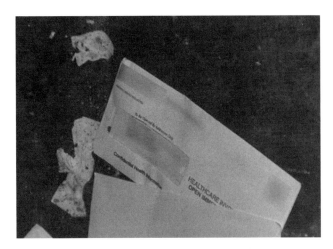

Curious, I walked around to the front of the building to check the tenant listing. Sure enough, the building directory listed the name of the healthcare provider I had seen stamped on the discarded envelopes. At that moment I knew that this was not a careless patient, but rather a careless healthcare provider.

I vaguely remembered something about legislation that threatened stiff penalties for healthcare providers that leaked patient information. A later Google search (yes, Google, and not Yahoo, thanks) revealed that the amendment to the Internal Revenue Service code of 1986, known by the acronym HIPAA (the Health Insurance Portability & Accountability Act) dealt with patient privacy. Specifically, it accounts for the "Protection of confidentiality and security of health data through setting and enforcing standards" and threatens fines of up to $250,000 for blatant abuses of its suggested standards. Although I knew this was not a quarter-million-dollar offense, I knew someone somewhere would probably be ticked off to know what this company was up to.

So did you tell them?

I have a feeling I'll be putting this sidebar in just about every chapter, but it bears repeating. I see this kind of near-criminal negligence all the time, but I hardly ever report it. I know from a moral standpoint that I should, but I have rotten luck reporting my finds. I've been scolded, threatened with legal action and harassed one too many times for trying to do the right thing. So for now, I'm out of the reporting game. Instead, I use the edited versions of these photos in my books and talks to raise awareness about the seriousness of the problem. At least in this way, these photos can serve some sort of positive end.

So what's the solution? First, raise awareness about the importance of trash. Signs like the one in the next photo are a nice reminder.

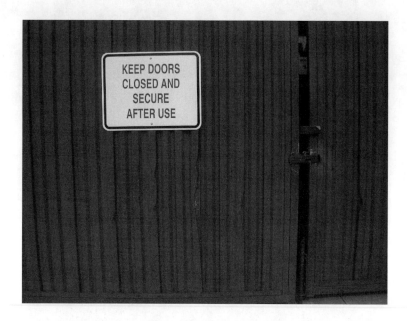

A lock to secure the dumpster gate is also a nice touch.

Even if this gate were locked, a motivated dumpster diver would just hop the fence. A gate lock combined with a dumpster lock isn't a half-bad idea, but when it comes to clamping down on dangerous dumpster docs, the golden rule is to shred everything. But shredding is a subjective word. There are lots of varieties of shredders, each of which provides a different level of security. A general-purpose strip-cut shredder will shred documents into vertical strips which can be easily reassembled. A cross cut shredder will cut the vertical strips horizontally. The smaller the resultant shred, the harder it is to reassemble the document. For example, a basic strip-cut shredder cuts documents into 1/8" by 1 1/8" pieces, like the ones shown in this photo.

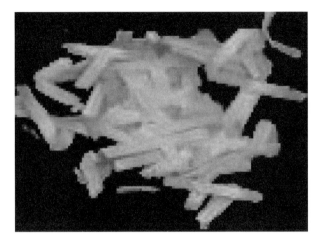

A top of the line, ultra-aggressive scanner will obliterate documents into 1 mm × 5 mm dust particles (shown in the next photo) that would frustrate even the world's best spy agencies.

Table 1.1 lists shredder specifications from least secure to most secure.

Table 1.1 Shredder Specifications

Type	Shred size	Purpose
Strip cut	3/8"	General documents
Cross cut	3/8" × 1 1/2" – 3 3/8"	General Documents
Strip cut	1/4" – 1/8"	Sensitive documents
Strip cut	1/16"	Confidential documents
Cross cut	1/8" × 1–1/8"	Confidential documents
Cross cut	1/16" × 5/8"	Secret Documents
Cross cut	1/32" × 1/2"	US DoD and Canadian RCMP rated Top Secret documents
Cross-cut	1/26" × 1/5" (1 mm × 5 mm)	Highest security level backed by U.S. government

A decent "micro-cut" shredder from an office supply store will cost around $200, and can cut paper, CDs and even credit cards into 3/32 × 5/16 pieces, for better than average security. Generally speaking, you'll get what you pay for. Whatever you chose, anything's better than putting documents in the trash in one piece, or laying them in the parking lot.

It's also smart to know what's in your trash before the bad guys do. If you're in charge of security for your company, consider at least a weekly visit to your dumpster. Get a feel for what's being tossed and what condition it's in when it lands in the big green box. If you're a consumer looking to protect your privacy, get a personal shredder and have a discussion with your family members about what should be shredded before being thrown away. If your family refuses to comply, you might consider relocating them. If they are not particularly noisy, you might find another great use for a dumpster with a lock on the lid.

(just kidding!)

Chapter 2

Tailgating

Hackers and Ninja go together like…smart people and stealthy assassins. OK, in reality, they really don't go well together at all unless you have a really smart ninja or a really deadly hacker, in which case we're more talking about ninja hackers, which in an entirely different breed. Don't even get me started about pirate ninja hackers. But I digress. Hackers and ninja both like wearing black, and they do share the ability to slip inside a building and blend with the shadows. They can also both do that smoke trick—the one that lets them pass through walls unscathed, engulfed by a cool-looking (but smelly) cloud of smoke. Impossible, you say? Hardly. Read on as I reveal yet another bit of pure, no-tech hacker (ninja) magic.

P.S. – I humbly apologize to my Bujinkan brothers and sisters for the stereotypical (but culturally relevant) description of the ninja.

Introduction to Tailgating

Tailgating simply means following an authorized person into a building—basically, riding on their coattails. When I suggested tailgating into a veritable fortress, Vince opted for the washcloth trick. His idea was better given the situation, but tailgating is still one of the best no-tech methods for gaining access to a secured building. Tailgating has become a household term, meaning it's a common problem.

Years ago, I was tasked with a physical assessment against a state government facility. The facility was split into two distinct areas: an open area to accommodate the general public and a restricted area for state employees. We were tasked with entering the restricted area and gaining access to the closed computer network inside. Our initial reconnaissance revealed that the open and restricted areas were connected, but an armed guard stood watch over the connecting hallway. The front door to the secured area was similarly protected. Doors armed with swipe card readers (none of which appeared vulnerable to the washcloth trick) protected each of the side doors. To make matters worse for my team, armed guards in marked vehicles patrolled the parking lots.

Although at first discouraged by the heavy security, we kept up our surveillance and eventually hit pay dirt. Huddled around a side entrance to the secured area, we spotted a group of employees chatting away while having a smoke. I knew immediately we had found our way in. We headed to the nearest gas station where I bought a pack of cigarettes and a lighter.

I had come prepared to social engineer my way into the building as a phone technician.[1] I wore cruddy jeans, work boots, and a white T-shirt with a phone company logo. I had a phone company employee badge clipped to my collar. My bright-yellow toolbox sported phone company logos and the clear top revealed a small stack of branded payphone info-strips. The toolbox was filled with phone test equipment. A battered hardhat completed the look.

The official-looking getup was, of course, a complete fabrication. I downloaded the phone company logo from the Internet. I printed the T-shirt myself using iron-on transfer paper. I printed the badge on my home printer and laminated it with a $2 kit. The payphone strips were liberated from some local payphones. The phone test gear

---

[1] Of course, the phone company I emulated had no part in this. I have no affiliation with them, and this attack in no way reflects a security problem with that particular phone company. Neither my company nor I endorse this kind of behavior except in conjunction with an authorized security test. And please don't full-body tackle every poor phone technician you spot in the hallway.

was legitimate, collected from various sources for just such an occasion. I found the hardhat abandoned on the side of the road. Its battered condition made it more convincing.

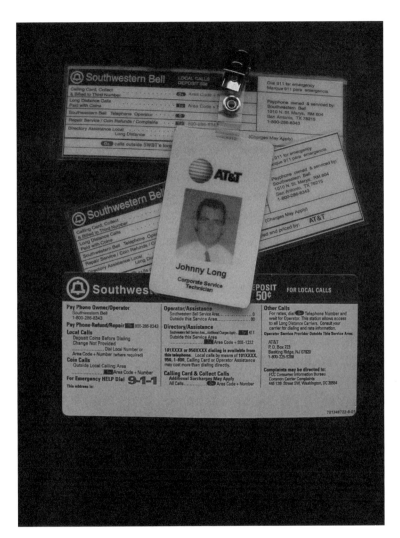

Approaching the group of smokers would have been a bad idea, regardless of how good an actor I turned out to be. If they watched me approach from the parking lot, they would consider me an outsider. If instead they came out of the building and found me already there, halfway through a smoke, they might assume I had come *out* of the building for a break.

After the group of smokers headed back inside, I hurried to the side door and lit up a cigarette. Two employees eventually came out and began talking between themselves.

I nodded casually and joined in their small talk. They chattered about company politics and I nodded at appropriate moments, making sure to blow smoke up into the air every now and then to convince them of my familiarity with cigarettes. I grunted about how the phone system had been acting up lately. They laughed and agreed (lucky for me) and I tried not to gag on the cigarette, wondering the whole time if I was turning as green as I felt. As they put out their smokes, they swiped their badges to return inside. I flicked my cigarette into the road—which is a corporate smoker faux pas–and held the door open for them. They thanked me for the kind gesture and I filed in behind them. Let me say that again. They *thanked me* for holding the door for them despite the fact that I had just broken into their building because of them. Once inside I had my way with the facility.

I made my way through the building and was never challenged. At one point, I even walked through the security office. The receptionist looked surprised to see me until I pointed to an empty desk and told her the phone was broken. She wasn't sure whether the phone was broken or not but she let me in. After all, I was the phone guy. I plopped my toolbox on the desk, picked up the phone and heard a dial tone. I shook my head, put the phone back on the cradle and lifted my toolbox off the desk, along with a stack of important-looking papers. I left the office grumbling about stupid work orders and how they always give me the wrong jack number and how it always made me look like an idiot. The receptionist giggled and told me to come back any time. I think she liked me. It was probably the helmet.

All in all, it was a good day. We popped yet another fortress with a series of simple, no-tech attacks. We left with piles of documents proving we had been inside, and my paperback-sized computer was loaded with hundreds of megabytes of sensitive State data. The employees never challenged me because they recognized the logo on my shirt and badge. Since the logos and the gear looked legit, I was probably who I appeared to be. But I had purposely played the role of a technician from the *wrong* phone company. The company I selected was a recognized data and voice service provider, but they didn't provide local hardware support. In layman's terms, even if I was an employee of that phone company, I had no business being in the facility, and even if I did, I wouldn't have been testing phone handsets.

It all boiled down to playing a convincing role. I used the age-old technique of tailgating to gain initial access to the building and then threw in a healthy dose of social engineering to schmooze everyone I ran into inside the building. Every employee took me at face value, even though any one of them could have put an immediate end to the break-in.

The phone technician gag isn't the only one at my disposal. Depending on the situation, I could have played the role of a delivery person, an electrician, a plumber, an elevator repairman or any other kind of service person. The choices are endless. All I need to do is be in the right place at the right time, present a convincing demeanor, and dress the part. Finding the right place and time takes patience. Schmoozing takes practice.

Dressing the part takes a bit more work, but even this is relatively simple. Let's take a look at what's required to get the right look.

Dressing the Part

Getting a photo helps. At first, I had trouble with this. Thinking people would get weirded out by my stalker ways, I remember I would did just about everything in my power to keep them from catching me in the act. I captured this photo of a phone service technician while driving.

Check out the perfectly focused stickers on my window (and yes, avid no-tech hacker, I drove a Honda at the time). To make matters worse, the guy saw me take his picture, and turned to watch as I drove past. He probably made a mental note of my license plate number and called it in to the local phone technician stalker hotline. So much for stealth. Once I even stepped off the sidewalk into a row of bushes to snag a quality covert photo of an approaching delivery guy. The photo didn't turn out, but at least I made a new friend. The delivery guy was nice enough to help me out of the prickly holly thicket.

Eventually I learned to follow my own advice and now I opt for a simpler approach–I just *ask* my target for permission to snap a few photos. I ask politely (avoiding those stalker vibes) and most people are more than happy to oblige me. In some cases, I make up a story about my kid liking big trucks, and ask if my target would mind posing for a quick photo. After, all, who's going to deny a little kid happiness? The delivery guy shown in the next (heavily blurred) photo was extremely accommodating. I got a photo of his truck, his outfit and even his employee badge—more than enough detail to pull together a convincing delivery-guy persona.

Don't shoot the messenger!

So the delivery guy let me take his picture. Should he be fired, or even reprimanded if I use his photo to break into some place dressed like him? Hardly. If I can wander around inside a target building dressed as a delivery guy, helping myself to sooper-secret documents, there's a problem with my target's security program. What it boils down to is that most folks take the world at face value. If an employee sees a familiar logo on a badge or a polo shirt, he or she will naturally assume I am who I appear to be. It's socially awkward to confront an unfamiliar person, but as I've already said—it takes just one vigilant person to stop my team in its tracks.

I'm sorry to say that I blurred everything recognizable from the next photo, but take my word for it; it's a delivery guy from another popular delivery company.

The phone technician in the next photo was hard at work on his laptop when I snapped the picture. Since he was so polite in allowing me to photograph him, I chose not to shoulder surf his session.

What if I told you one of the phone guys shown in the next photo was a phony? Would you be able to tell me which one?

Is the guy in the next photo a gas and electric technician or a hacker? He's got an official-looking hat with just the right gas and electric logos, and he's carrying an electronic gizmo. Considering this is exactly how many gas and electric employees dress when doing field work, you might never know the difference.

As a final example, consider the techie in the next photo. Scenes like this are relatively common in today's high-tech environments. He's obviously pondering a deep technical issue that mere mortals could never fully understand. It seemed rude to disturb him as he toiled away, so I just snapped some photos.

However, as the next photo shows, he's no ordinary techie. Yes, he's got his laptop jacked into an ATM machine.

Does this make him more suspicious that he was a moment ago? Probably not. Could he be a hacker? Maybe. The odds suggest that he's exactly who he appears to be—an ATM repair guy with an ID badge and everything. But doesn't every decent ATM hacker carry some sort of legitimate-looking badge?

When it comes time to bust your first potential hacker as a security-conscious citizen, you'll most likely have serious misgivings about the situation. Approaching any hard-core techie in mid-algorithm is a universally stupid idea. Techies get grumpy about stuff like that. Besides, he'll be really grumpy if you jack his flow and he turns out to be legitimately plugging away at his underpaying job. On the other hand, if this guy has the stones to hack an ATM smack-dab in the middle of a busy hallway, he's probably got no qualms about rattling off a bold-faced lie to get you to go away. If he's got real skill, he'll talk you out of *your* employee badge so he doesn't get hassled anymore as he tries to protect *your* bank account from evil ATM hackers.

Correctly assessing the situation can be dizzying, but fortunately you don't need to play vigilante. If you think something's up, tell someone who gets paid to care. Security guards, police officers, air marshals, mirror-shaded Secret Service agents and school crossing guards all care very deeply about protecting those in their charge. And even if they don't care about protecting anything but themselves, most of them enjoy the paycheck their work produces. So the odds are pretty good that if you tell them about a potential security threat, they'll either do something about it or get fired when that particular bad guy ends up robbing the place blind. Either way, it's better to allow them the opportunity to do their job rather than play full-time hall monitor. I'm sure you have better things to do than annoying innocent bystanders.

And to those in charge of security guards, police officers, air marshals, mirror-shaded Secret Service agents and school crossing guards: make sure your people are informed enough to know how to handle "visitors" and that they tend to not choose the plank instead of doing the right thing. And keep an eye out for situations that seem to invite tailgating. For example, the next photo shows a woman swiping into the secured door of a U.S. government facility.

The next photo shows the same door approximately ten seconds later.

After fifteen seconds or so, the door finally shut, allowing more than enough time for an intruder to slip through. The lady that swiped was nowhere to be found. Pay attention to these situations. The bad guys certainly do.

Real-World Tailgating Exercise

Tailgating describes the act of following an individual into a secured area, but getting in is only the beginning. Join me as I show you what a typical tailgating session looks like. I gained access to my target building by following an employee in through a side door. Although I tailgated behind the employee, I later realized the door wasn't even locked. It did, however sport an *Emergency Exit Only* sign. Once inside the building, I got my camera ready. As soon as I did, I found another employee wandering the hallway. I held the camera to my waist, and took the series of photos shown below.

The lady had a kind face and was very polite. I felt bad for snagging this rapid-fire series of photos that show the details of her lanyard and badge, but she wasn't the only security-unconscious employee. I captured several other badge shots while inside the building.

As I wandered the halls, I found this trash bag sitting outside a locked office door.

The clear bag revealed a pretty typical assortment of office garbage: banana peels, soda cans, paper plates and American Express bills.

Most of the offices inside the building were locked, protected by proximity card readers. Opting for the no-tech approach, I ignored these locked spaces and continued wandering. I took the next photo outside one office suite.

The phone wasn't nearly as interesting as it could have been. Instead of a handy personnel directory, it listed the calling features of the phone: call waiting, conference calling, call forwarding and call parking. The pile of mail, on the other hand, seemed very interesting. Adopting the hands-off approach, I didn't rifle through it, but the top envelope was another American Express bill.

As I continued to wander the hallways, I spotted an open door that looked like a janitor's closet. I angled myself to get a look inside, and froze in my tracks.

This was no janitor closet—this was a network closet. This holy grail of tailgaters was sitting before me, wide open and completely unattended. Not only that, but each of the consoles was logged in, allowing me to do whatever I wanted to the company's phone and computer network systems. I could have installed a backdoor, dropped a worm ("…a multi-headed worm to break an encryption and sniff out digital footprints throughout an encrypted network," as John Travolta in the movie *Swordfish* once said) or whatever I wanted. Or I could have opted for a less Hollywood approach and installed my own WAP or a hardware key logger. Either way, the company's phone calls, emails and confidential info were at my disposal, without having to leverage a single high-tech attack.

Although most facilities are much more security-conscious than this one, every single real-world attack I've launched in my professional career has involved some sort of no-tech hacking angle. Keep your eyes open as you walk through your everyday life, think like a hacker, and you'll begin to see these things as well.

Chapter 3

Shoulder Surfing

Dude. Surfing on your shoulder? Whoa. No, it's not a surfing-gymnastics mash up, but it is a sport—a hacker sport. Forget what you think you know about hackers eyeballing your password as you poke it out on your keyboard. We're talking about the X-Games version where hackers suck super-secret data of a laptop using only their minds. No psychic friends network here, just pure caffeinated hacker ingenuity. If you like having a screen on your laptop so you can see what you're working on, don't read this chapter. Because you might just want to rip your laptop's screen clean off when you experience shoulder surfing through the eyes of a no-tech hacker.

What is Shoulder Surfing?

Shoulder surfing is a classic no-tech attack that's been around about as long as shoulders themselves. It's a simple attack. All a bad guy does is peer over a victim's shoulder to see what he or she is up to. Back in the old days (before 1990 or so) this technique was used to snag calling card digits as a victim entered them into a public pay phone. A thief could reuse those digits to make free long distance calls, or sell them to others for less than market value. Although there are much easier ways to capture calling card digits these days, the skill of keypad monitoring still has many very practical uses. For example, consider the security screen below, presented at the cash register of an office supply store.

Like all the terminals located throughout the store (including many customer accessible terminals), this one prompts for an employee number and password. The kiosk allows access privileges based on the credentials entered. A manager will obviously have a higher level of access than an employee or a customer (who typically has no credentials). For certain transactions, such as the return of a high-value item, a manager login is required. As the next photo shows, a skilled keypad watcher (or cell phone video cam user) can capture the keystrokes as they are entered.

A no-tech hacker could then reuse those credentials at a customer terminal to do all sorts of interesting (read: nasty) things.

Keep Those Digits to Yourself

What's the point of requiring a pass code if you enter it in plain site of everyone? When entering sensitive data, create some sort of barrier between the keys and wandering eyes. This might require you to reposition your body, or create a shield with your spare hand. If you aren't willing to do this, why have a pass code at all?

Keypad data capture is still pretty old school, though. When the world went digital, shoulder surfers turned their glances from keypads to keyboards, hunting not for calling card numbers, but for passwords. This is no easy trick. Every time I try to pull it off, I'm reminded of the classic move *Sneakers*. The entire hacker "dream team" was baffled by video footage of a mathematician entering his password. Rewinding the footage, they eventually realized the password was indiscernible—the victim was just in the way. Fortunately, this chapter isn't about catching those fleeting passwords. It's about being observant and realizing that shoulder surfers have evolved beyond keyboard-watching.

Outside of the box

Before we get into actual shoulder surfing technique, let's first talk about how easy it is to profile a target by looking at the machine itself. Consider the traveler shown in the next photo.

A true techie would probably already have figured out the age and model of the IBM ThinkPad based solely on the design of the machine and the ports on the back. A hacker might swing around behind the machine to get a glimpse of the screen in an attempt to learn more about this target. But a decent no-tech hacker (or an astute observer) would instead check out the business card taped to the laptop lid which reveals the target's name, company, job title, address, office phone and cell phone number. The tape-on business card phenomenon is becoming quite the rage. I see them everywhere these days. Here's another one I captured in the wild.

A relative of the tape-on business card is the company-supplied inventory sticker. Many times these are simple tiny barcode stickers, but some (like the one shown in the next photo) are larger, and reveal quite a bit of information.

Check out the undisputed king of corporate stick-on I captured in the next photo.

Not only does this poor laptop sport a corporate inventory sticker, it's adorned with a corporate logo and a super-bright hot orange sign that screams "ultra sensitive" in English and what I guess is Chinese. Even an illiterate laptop thief might get the clue that this laptop is one worth stealing. This brings up an important point. While laptop stickers can be used to profile a victim, they can also serve to mark a laptop as valuable, making the owner a target for theft or physical violence. I'm reminded of the U.S. Government "Classified," "Secret," and "Top Secret" stickers which I've seen in the field. While I understand the practical value of these stickers in a mixed-classification government environment, I've seen way too many of them out in the wild. Even the benign "Unclassified" sticker is an indication that the device is used in or around government spaces, making the device a target for thieves, spies and UFO conspiracy theorists.

Say "No" to Stickers

Those stickers have got to go. If you're forced to have them on your gear, consider putting a sticky note over them when you're traveling. This will at least keep the sticker (and the information that can be inferred from it) hidden from too-curious eyes.

It's impossible to have a no-tech discussion about stickers without mentioning the most famous sticky of them all: the Post-It note. I can't tell you how many sticky notes I've seen in my travels. They often appear on monitors and desks and almost always contain interesting information a no-tech hacker can take advantage of. I discovered the machines below sitting unattended inside a fancy hotel's loading dock.

Pay no mind to the paperwork that fills every nook and cranny and nearly every square inch of wall space. Try to focus beyond the unlocked file cabinets and instead have a look at the computer systems and those gorgeous sticky notes. Most are useless to my eyes, but one contained what looked like login credentials, which (judging from the network cable) authenticate to the hotel network—the same network that serves the guest registration database. A no-tech hacker can gather plenty of information without touching a single machine or committing a single crime. And if someone catches him in the room? Well, he's just a confused guest in search of a bathroom. Good luck proving otherwise.

Great Locations for Should Surfing

There are many great locations for shoulder surfing, but some are better than others. First, let's talk about airports.

The first shoulder-surfing opportunity at an airport occurs during check-in, especially at the self-service kiosks, which we talk more about in Chapter 9. Check-in kiosks clearly display information such as the traveler's name, destination, seating assignment and frequent flier number during the check-in process. Security checkpoints also offer the unique (and unsettling) opportunity to shoulder-surf TSA agents as they go about their business.

Since hanging around security checkpoints taking photos of TSA agents isn't such a smart idea, a no-tech hacker will inevitably head for the executive lounge, where he'll either legitimately enter or social engineer his way inside. These lounges are often packed with high-profile people doing high-profile things, most of whom are oblivious to shoulder surfers.

There's great fun to be had at the gates as well, thanks to the back-to-back seating arrangement and the bustle and distraction made by a constant stream of weary travelers. The photo below was taken in this sort of environment.

Despite the awkward angle and horrible lighting, the screen is still perfectly readable (I have blurred the screen to protect the user's crystal-clear Outlook email session). Semi-private kiosks provide even better lighting, making it much easier for a surfer that's quite a distance away. The Vice President of Acquisitions shown in the next photo was oblivious to my presence as he pecked out a confidential inter-department email.

Lounges in and around airports offer great surfing opportunities as well, as shown in the next photo.

Although airport systems are hardly ever a target for most no-tech hackers, it's impossible not to notice unattended airport personnel workstations. The airline Sabre system shown in the next photo is practically begging to be tinkered with.

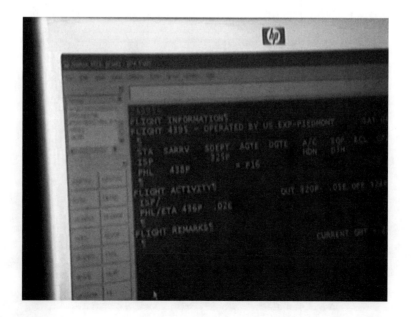

Coffee shops are another favorite hangout for shoulder surfers, as shown in the next few photos.

It seems that the more comfortable the environment, the less wary it's patrons tend to be. I've personally seen everything from architectural designs (shown in the next photo) to confidential emails to government proposal documents being edited in coffee shops, and other no-tech hackers have told me tales of even more interesting things.

Business lounges offer great opportunities for kiosk hackers (discussed in Chapter 9) but also for shoulder surfers, as shown in the next photo.

If it's important enough to work on in a hotel business lounge, it's probably pretty important. Shoulder surfers know this. Keep aware.

Keep It Secret, Keep It Safe

Sorry for the blatantly geeky Lord of The Rings quote, but Gandalf's got it right. Keep your private stuff from public consumption. Don't work on your personal stuff in public spaces, and don't make yourself a target. Be aware of the profile you are presenting, and tone it down if necessary. If you've got to work on private stuff in public, consider a laptop privacy filter (try a Google search for "laptop privacy filter"). Of course bear in mind that an experienced shoulder surfer will see a privacy filter and rightly assume you're working on something sensitive. Because of this, the mere existence of a filter can make you or your machine a target. Did I mention leaving the private stuff out of public spaces? That's your best bet.

Electronic Deduction

Information is certainly more valuable than hardware, and professional thieves understand this. Although an amateur thief may have a decent understanding of the relative value of something like a laptop based on it age and hardware specifications, a professional will often use no-tech techniques to determine the relative value of the data stored on a machine by profiling the machine's user. We've already looked at a few interesting external clues, but the best way to profile a machine's owner is to get a look at the screen.

StankDawg (http://www.stankdawg.com) released a paper entitled *The Art of Electronic Deduction* (http://www.docdroppers.org/wiki/index.php?title=The_Art_of_ Electronic_Deduction) which explored the methods an attacker can use to glean information from interesting electronic sources. Taking a cue from his paper, check out the photo below of a temporarily unattended laptop I spotted in a coffee shop.

I have altered the image to keep the owner's company name confidential, but by using the information on the screen, an accomplished no-tech hacker can glean an awful lot of information. For starters, the desktop background indicates that the laptop is running Windows XP Professional. Other aesthetic clues such as the Start button configuration back this up. The operating system of a machine is a necessary piece of information a technical attacker can use to determine the type of attack to launch. Generally, an attacker would need to analyze a series of network packet responses to determine this information, but in this case that is unnecessary—it is unlikely the laptop's owner has installed another operating system's desktop background. Focusing on the icons on the desktop, we can immediately deduce the company the user works for as one icon (blurred in the above image) spells it out clearly. The icons below help us deduce even more.

The word *sales* indicates that this is some sort of sales software, but a Google search reveals that SalesLogix is the leader in mid-market CRM (customer relationship management) software. The search goes on to say that SalesLogix is "the most powerful sales tool on the Web." We can confidently deduce that the owner is in a sales position. The icons below refer to *SAP*, a common business software solution provider.

The existence of the SAP logon client indicates the logon credentials for the service may be installed on the laptop as well. If a thief were to make off with this machine, there's a decent chance he or she may be able to log into the company's SAP system using stored credentials. The icon below is titled *SecuRemote*.

A Google search reveals that *SecuRemote* is a virtual private network (VPN) client. As with the SAP logon software, all or part of the VPN credentials may reside on the laptop, allowing an adversary access to the corporate network. At the very least, the mere existence of a particular brand of VPN is valuable information to a technical attacker.

The icons below reveal that Palm personal digital assistant (PDA) software has been installed on the machine. The owner probably owns a Palm device, and the contents of that device are most likely backed up or synced to the laptop.

The icon below reveals the existence of the AT&T Global Network Client.

Again, this network client may have cached credentials, which might allow an adversary in possession of the laptop to log in as the machine's owner. An unfortunately named icon is shown below.

I can only hope that this document does not contain any sort of actual access code. That would make a bad guy's job *way* too easy.

Desktop icons provide a great deal of information, but a technically savvy attacker can learn even more by looking at other details on the screen. For example, what information can you determine by looking at the taskbar below?

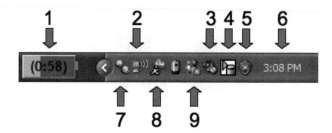

This taskbar itself reveals an awful lot of information. The layout reveals that we're looking at a modern version of Windows, most likely Windows XP. But each of the icons has meaning as well. How many can you identify? Here's what each of the icons represents.

1. This is the battery indicator, which shows this machine is a laptop, and that there are fifty-eight minutes of battery power remaining. We can tell that the machine is not plugged into a power source because there is no electrical plug icon next to the battery.

2. This icon reveals that the machine is connected to (and communicating with) a wireless access point. The third icon.

3. This icon shows that the system speakers are muted.

4. This is the IBM *Hard Drive Active Protection* program icon. It reveals that the machine is an IBM laptop, and that no system shocks have been detected (the machine has not been dropped recently).

5. This icon represents the Microsoft Security Center, which is currently disabled—meaning that the security level of the machine is less than optimal and may be vulnerable to attack. This is also verification that the machine is running a modern version of XP.

6. This is the system clock, which is set to 3:08 P.M. This information can be correlated with the current local time to help determine the time zone the owner originated in. If it's not set to where they are, it's set to where they're from.

7. This icon belongs to the Trillian instant messaging program. The Trillian website (www.ceruleanstudios.com) describes the program as "a fully featured, stand-alone, skinnable chat client that supports AIM, ICQ, MSN, Yahoo Messenger, and IRC." It goes on to say that "It provides capabilities not possible with original network clients, while supporting standard features…" In layman's terms, Trillian is an instant messaging client replacement. The style of the icon indicates that Trillian is connected and logged in.

8. This is the ever-popular AIM (AOL Instant Messaging) icon, and its style indicates that the program is connected to a server and that the user is logged in.

9. This icon belongs to Microsoft Instant Messenger (MSN), and its style reveals that the program is running, but the user is not logged on.

10. If it seems odd that this person is running Trillian, AIM, and MSN all at the same time, you've picked up on an interesting point. The Trillian software makes the AIM and MSN clients redundant. So beyond the fact that this person is probably looking for love in all the wrong places he or she is probably not all that technical—there seems to be little reason to be connected with both AIM and Trillian at the same time. The mere fact that these clients are in active use gives an observer grounds for more research since both MSN and AIM require users to sign up for an account online, and create a personal profile, which may contain personal information. Yahoo's instant messenger client is currently the most bloated in terms of add-ons and created online profiles. A Yahoo user has to be very careful not to reveal too much personal information.

Instant Messaging Profile Pitfalls

We could do an entire book on the privacy implications of using instant messenger programs. When signing up for an account, a new user creates all sorts of data trails that a hacker or identity thief could uncover. While we don't have the page space to go into all the potential pitfalls here, just understand that poorly configured IM clients are bad news if you're concerned about your privacy.

An online investigation of this IM user would at least require a username. If a chat window is left open, like the one provided by StankDawg below, the user's name is in plain site at the top of the window.

Armed with the logged-in user name, an observer could start an online information gathering exercise to profile the machine's owner. This exercise would include a search of the target's buddy's information as well. Armed with a well-populated buddy list (like the one shown below, also provided by StankDawg), an observer could delve deep into the personal life of a target, beginning with the least privacy-conscious buddy's profile first.

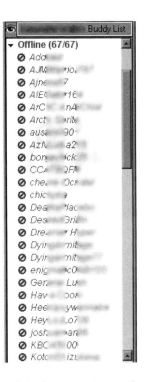

Sometimes the names on a buddy list aren't nearly as important as the appearance of the buddy list itself. StankDawg provides the Yahoo Instant Messenger buddy list show below.

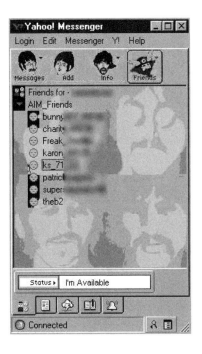

It's obvious that this user is a Beatles fan. A social engineer could leverage this information as a conversation starter. As StankDawg says, an observer can create a "preponderance of evidence" which uses seemingly useless coincidental evidence to build a profile of a target. When these bits of evidence come from multiple sources—screen shots, body language, dress, mannerisms, etc—an observer can build an amazingly accurate profile of a potential target.

But any profile built this way can be flawed. The best no-tech hacker realizes this and does not discount a single piece of evidence. Consider the expanded taskbar shown below. It is an expanded version of the instant messenger junkie's taskbar we discussed above.

There are lots of interesting icons that weren't visible before, but the one marked with the arrow is particularly revealing. The onion icon represents Vidalia, a package that incorporates Tor (The Onion Router) and Privoxy, two tools used to anonymize a user's Internet activity. A user surfing the Web with Privoxy Tor enabled surfs in complete and utter anonymity. Remote Web sites can't tell where the user is coming from, and anyone sniffing the local network traffic can't see where the user is going. This tiny icon, consisting of no more than forty pixels, tells a great deal about the user of this machine. The user is no half-witted web surfer who doesn't know his AIM from his MSN. At the very least, he or she is a privacy advocate, and at the worst he or she is up to something nefarious. This speculation could be misguided, but the best of no-tech hackers can accurately distill all these interesting tidbits into fact and then make a decision based on those facts—all in a dizzyingly short period of time.

Gah! It's all too much! Help me!

The best defense is to remain aware when traveling. Don't put yourself in situations that invite shoulder surfers. Position your back to the wall when using your machine, and never leave your machine unattended. Don't wear company logos. Remove extraneous markings and information from your mobile computing devices, especially if your company name might entice an adversary. The tech support folks in your organization can probably provide you a long list of tech things to avoid when traveling. Follow their advice.

Electronic deduction is definitely an art. We could fill page after page with the topic but understand what we're getting at here—literally every square inch of your screen contains something of interest to a no-tech hacker. If you've got something on your machine that might tempt a thief or no-tech hacker, keep it out of the public eye. There's no sense making yourself a target.

Killer Real-Life Surfing Sessions

Military Intelligence

The best way to explain what goes on in the mind of a no-tech hacker is to show you. In this section, we'll take a look at some real-world shoulder surfing sessions. The first example centers on the guy in the next photo.

It's obvious that he's a member of the U.S. military. The insignia and patches on his uniform reveal quite a bit, especially to those with military knowledge. While certain adversaries might take an interest in him because of his military affiliation, any no-tech hacker can learn an awful lot by looking at the gear that surrounds this guy.

For starters it's obvious he's a Mac user. He's using a Mac PowerBook and his white headphones are an iPod signature item. The off-screen Mac Addict magazine seals the deal—he's a bona fide Apple fan-boy. Closer examination reveals that he's also a gamer.

The icons in his dock (shown below) mean that he's installed World of Warcraft (WoW) and Ventrillo voice communication software.

A social engineer might use this knowledge to his advantage, choosing to either engage him in a WoW or Windows-bashing conversation. But many no-tech hackers will avoid social engineering unless it's absolutely necessary. By moving in closer to surf this guy, an adversary can learn much, as we'll see.

But I have to say I am surprised to find this particular target with his back to the world and his headphones on, especially considering the "RoadWarrior" guide I discovered recently.

This guide includes a handy tear-off wallet card which reminds "road warriors" to "Ensure against public display of content: Shoulder Surfing." The guide also goes on to advocate being "a wary and alert traveler."

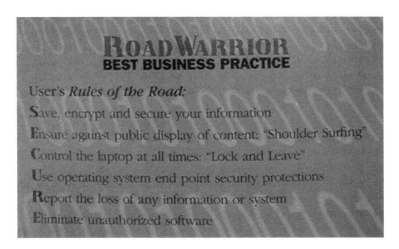

Still, as you can tell from the next photo, moving in on this guy is simple, thanks to his blaring headphones and his corner-facing position.

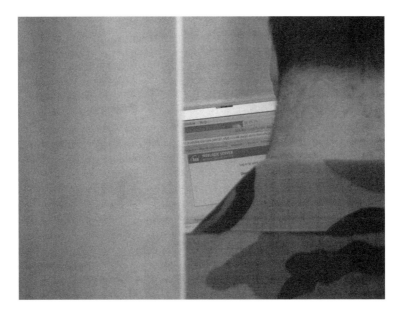

As it turns out, he's not casually surfing the Web—he's logging into the administrative console of a BEA WebLogic server. Given that Weblogic is heavyweight industrial-grade software, it's safe to assume that he's busy with work—perhaps even official

U.S. Government business. As he typed his credentials, I made a quick adjustment to my camera and took another photo. The flash fired, and the target turned around sharply, finally noticing me. I looked down at the camera and rubbed my eyes, pretending to be blinded by my own flash. He shrugged and returned to his work, convinced, I assume, that I was some kind of digital camera newbie just figuring out the ropes. This road warrior did not *want* to assume I was taking a picture of him. That, of course could create all sorts of unpleasantness for him. So he did what most portable computer users do—he assumed the best, and went back to his work. This makes the job of a no-tech hacker even easier.

Throw Down!

I'm not suggesting you body tackle every oddball that might be shoulder surfing you. What I would suggest is that you close your machine if you think you're a target and become interested in something else, like sipping your coffee. Most no-tech hackers will know they've been busted and move along. If they do, keep a casual eye on them as they leave and try to get a good look at them and their car/bike/skateboard/Segway before they bail. When they've cleared out take a look at what you were working on, consider all of it compromised, and act accordingly. If your surfer doesn't bail after you close your lid, keep an eye on him or her anyhow. If he or she continues acting suspiciously, do something about it. Inform a manager, security guard or hall monitor. Do *something*. If that something involves physical violence, just don't tell the judge it was my idea.

Airliner Espionage

Our next example takes place at 30,000 feet on board a commercial airliner. Airplanes are tough places to shoulder surf because a surfer is generally limited to checking out the people around him or in the aisles surrounding the rest rooms, where passengers tend to hang out. Hovering over a stranger's shoulder anywhere else gets the undercover air marshal all nervous.

Since I hardly ever get any sleep while traveling (who can sleep with all the no-tech hacking to do?) I was awake to catch the late-night laptop party happening in the next row.

At first, I wasn't all that interested since I was in the opposite window seat, and the aisle seat next to me was occupied by an awake and over-caffeinated stranger. Still, when my neighbor stood up to go to the bathroom, I couldn't resist the wide-open photo opportunity. I turned off my flash, and took the next photo.

The photo was boring and the angle was too sharp, but as I scoped the guy, I realized that his entire demeanor screamed *government*. His wing tips were nice, but not too nice. His binder was decidedly Government Issue, and the glance I stole of his laptop bag revealed what looked like a government insignia of some sort. I watched disinterested for a few more moments until my shot-blocking neighbor returned. As he settled into his seat, he grabbed the in-flight magazine and started flipping through it. Figuring my game of surf-the-fed was at an end; I closed my camera and tried to find something better to do. I remember feeling relieved. Despite how good the session might be, surfing is still hard work. But as fate would have it, the game wasn't quite over—it was just beginning. The fed pulled out a notebook stuffed with interesting-looking paperwork. Getting a shot of that paperwork from the other side of the plane seemed tricky, but I held up my jacket to form an impromptu curtain, flicked the zoom and took a quick shot. No one seemed to notice.

More paperwork surfaced and I felt drawn by it. Although I'm not usually the government employee stalker type, I just knew this guy was working on something significant, and he didn't seem to care who watched him do it. I accepted his invitation and eventually caught a glimpse of a juicy header page. I couldn't get my camera out fast enough to snap the next photo.

The page (written in monster header font) read *Government Systems EW/SIGINT 2006 Strategic Plan*. Any amateur GoogleDork can tell you that "EW/SIGINT" means Electronic Warfare Signals Intelligence in military-speak. I felt my pulse quicken as I realized I was at 30,000 feet surfing the government's 2006 strategic plan for their electronic warfare signals intelligence something-or-other. I immediately stopped taking photos of my careless Fed friend and have been stalked by black helicopters ever since. I'm not too freaked out by that though, because now I know how to disable their electronic systems with a cheap digital watch and a patch of duct tape. Although sometimes at night my wife complains about the noise.

Robbing a Bank

With their electronic and physical security systems, banks are in the Top Five list of high-security targets. But one thing I've come to learn in this business is that even the best security systems share a common flaw: lazy human beings. I really had no intention of robbing the bank in the next photo when I strolled by it.

But as I walked past the front door, I caught a glimpse of the bank manager sitting in his corner office working on his computer system. I stopped in my tracks and turned to look at him through the window. Although he was in my line of sight, he didn't seem to notice me. I pulled out my (ever present) camera, backed up a step and snapped the next photo.

Oblivious to my presence, he turned around and began working on some paperwork at his desk. Still standing in the same position, I zoomed my camera in and grabbed a photo of his screen. I reviewed the image and realized that the camera had focused on his blinds, making the on-screen text completely unreadable. The manager continued working at his desk, so I adjusted my focal length (which took me a while because it's something I rarely have to do) and snapped a few more photos. Eventually, I got a few like the one below, which captured the screen text in perfect clarity. (The area inside the box is unaltered—I have blurred the rest to protect the innocent.)

As I stood there reading the bank manager's screen on my camera's LCD screen, I had a realization–stealing money from a bank is *so lame*. The information housed by a bank is worth so much more than the actual liquid assets they have in the vault. Professional criminals and amateur identity thieves alike could easily liquidate a bank's information stores to reap millions of dollars in cold, hard (unmarked) cash, with far less risk than storming a lobby and taking hostages. I wondered how much one screen of personal information would fetch. As I pondered how rich I would be if I was one of the bad guys, the banker stood up from his desk and left his office unattended. I fiddled with the zoom again and snapped a few photos of the contents of his desk. Eventually the zoom settings cooperated and I captured a clear image of his paperwork.

I never imagined how simple it could be for a no-tech hacker to siphon information from a bank. I scoped the rest of his office and snapped some more photos like this next one.

I checked the images and found them all to be crystal-clear. After a few moments, the manager strolled back through his office door. As I stood there with my camera at eye level, aimed at his guest table, I wondered if I had liberated enough info to sell on the black market to pay my bail money. It hadn't dawned on me that he might actually have gone to alert security about his new voyeuristic hacker friend. He shuffled around the desk, adjusted his belt and his pants and plopped down into his overstuffed chair without casting me a single glance.

I waited a few stressful moments, fully expecting to be tasered by a trigger-happy bank rent-a-cop. It never happened. I turned and continued past the office, nearly bumping into an office employee out on a smoke break. The employee never noticed me—he was busy chatting on his cell phone, right outside the banker's office. I suddenly realized that the banker "tuned out" everyone lingering outside his office. He had gotten so used to passers by that now everyone outside his window (including no-tech hacker types with cameras) was a harmless irrelevance. Security guards often suffer from the same problem after watching a video monitor for hours on end. They get so used to nothing happening that when something finally does, they miss it.

Can I Get a Copy of Those Photos?

Uhmm, no. Let me say it again. I'm not one of the bad guys. If I were, I'd be either rich or in Cell Block 13 married to Bubba. As such, I've got a pretty high ethical standard and am only in the business of raising awareness about the threats I leverage in my professional life. I'm also not in the business of addressing every single potential threat I witness, like this bank problem. Most folks don't take too kindly to the likes of me poking at their stuff.

As I stood at the teller desk during a later (legitimate) visit to the bank, my eyes meandered to the tech gear behind the counter. I pulled out my camera phone and snapped the photo below.

The tiny, blurred, heavily altered (protecting my rear-end) photo of a printer isn't much to look at. Sorry. But I've included it for two reasons. First, it's possible to take a picture just about anywhere these days—even airport customs desks where the armed guards hang out and all the signs say "No Photographs."

The second reason I included the printer photo is not because of the printer itself, but because of the stickers on the top (blurred, etc, etc) which clearly list the name and telephone number of the I.T. company the bank uses for computer support. If you think that dressing up as the computer repairman only works in the movies, think again. I've done it successfully several times. And when I've done it I didn't have the luxury of knowing who the actual I.T. support company was.

Robbing Banks in Uganda, Africa

While on a recent mission trip to Uganda, Africa (see http://johnny.ihackstuff.com/uganda) I wasn't exactly in the no-tech hacker mindset. It was, after all, a wholly different place from my home in the United States. But as I stood at the ATM machine at one of the largest banks in Jinja, I couldn't help but notice that the bank had a strange sort of open iron fencing above each of the locked doors. Amused, I snapped the photo below.

As I looked at the photo in my viewfinder, my mind reeled with all the potential security problems this fencing presented. My mentor Vince would have had a field day with this type of setup. The coat hanger trick could probably be used to unlatch the door or block a security camera, or… My thoughts were interrupted by a nudge and I spun around. An unhappy-looking gentleman with a menacing looking rifle stood behind me. "No pictures. Put the camera away," he said, almost (but not quite) politely.

The rifle was impressive, and the uniform was even more impressive. His hat and lapel were emblazoned with a logo that read "Tight Security." The irony was thick. Here I was in a place that many would consider third-world, and I was facing perhaps the best security I had ever witnessed anywhere. I glanced over the man's shoulder and suddenly noticed that three other guards, similarly armed and dressed, were along the bank's outer perimeter.

"Friggin' sweet," I said with a smile.

The guard's expression sagged, his smile faded. "Put away the camera," he said.

I looked down and realized I still held the camera. I cleared my throat and put the camera away.

Friggin' sweet.

Chapter 4

Physical Security

Locks are serious business and lock technicians are true engineers, most backed with years of hands-on experience. But what happens when you take the age-old respected profession of the locksmith and sprinkle it with hacker ingenuity? That's when the magic shows up again. The locks you and I once depended on fall victim to no-tech tools like fountain pens, electric flossers and toilet paper rolls; the combo locks that protected our stuff with tens of thousands of combinations fall in less than three minutes with no tools at all; the locks the government mandates we use on our luggage surrender to tools made of soda cans shims and discarded shards of plastic; and most disturbing of all we find that the gun locks that protect our children from harm snap open after clever wielding of a drinking straw. Once our locks fall to these trivial attacks, we count on our cameras, motion sensors and alarm systems, only to see them trivially bypassed as well. Sound serious? It is. We'll be joined by some of the world's foremost experts in the field, and we'll have some fun along the way but I'm sure you'll sense the sky over the security landscape darken as you make your way through the longest and most in-depth chapter yet. Welcome to the world of physical security, no-tech hacking style.

Introduction

I remember my first physical assessment. I imagined myself picking locks and disabling electronic surveillance systems. I imagined myself as that marine in the movie Aliens, Hudson (played by Bill Paxton), frantically noodling with wires in an electronic lock, trying to get his team inside to safety. Although I ended up breaking into all sorts of amazing places in real life—and eventually did bypass a number of electronic surveillance systems—I never had to resort to picking a single lock. Simpler techniques always prevailed. In this section, I'll share some of the no-tech techniques that both beginner criminals and the most seasoned pros rely on.

Lock Bumping

Lock picking is a technical exercise. It requires knowledge of lock mechanics and internals, and perfecting the technique takes quite a bit of practice. *Lock bumping*, on the other hand, falls firmly into the no-tech hacking category. The technique involves the use of *bump keys*, which are keys fashoned by cutting a key blank so that each cut is made to a maximum depth and the tip and shoulder have been filed down by approximately half a millimeter. To a trained eye, bump keys have a very distinct look. The cuts are too uniform, as shown in the photo below.

(Permission Granted by Toool—The Open Organization Of Lockpickers)

The technique works by inserting a bump key into a lock and tapping the key while turning it slightly in the lock. The bottom internal pins in the lock are nudged, transferring momentum to the pins sitting above them. As the top pins fly upwards, the bottom pins remain down. When the pins separate, the cylinder can be turned, and if done correctly, the lock will open. Bypassing a lock with a bump key takes much less skill than picking the lock with a traditional lock pick set or electronic pick device. This means that just about anyone can compromise a vulnerable lock when armed with a proper bump key. For more information on prevention and identification of vulnerable locks, see the references mentioned in the sidebar, or contact a professional locksmith or security provider.

Treasure Trove of Bumping Info

Lock Bumping has been around for many years, but has gained popularity because of several recent works. Marc Tobias's book *Locks, Safes, and Security*[1] is an excellent reference book for professionals, and includes a great piece on bumping (or "rapping," as it is sometimes called). His Web site (http://security.org) and alerts page (http://security.org/dial-90/alerts.htm) are also excellent resources. If you're looking for more accessible material, I highly recommend the awesome whitepaper "Bumping Locks" (http://www.toool.nl/bumping.pdf) by Barry Wels and Rop Gonggrijp of Toool, The Open Organization Of Lockpickers, and their awesome video workshop *What the Bump?* at http://connectmedia.waag.org/toool/whatthebump.wmv. The Toool Web site (www.toool.nl) has a ton of resources and videos I highly recommend.

Shimming Padlocks (*With Deviant Ollam*)

Shimming is the use of a thin tool to bypass or disable the latch mechanism within a lock. By working a sheet or blade of material (typically steel or aluminum) into the right areas within a lock, components responsible for retaining a shackle or bolt can be forced aside, allowing the mechanism to release. This is typically only possible when critical elements of the lock rely exclusively on spring pressure to click into place.

---

[1] M.W. Tobias. *Locks, Safes and Security: An International Police Reference Two Volumes*, Charles C Thomas Pub Ltd, 2000.

In essence, shimming causes the lock to operate as if it were being *secured* by the user. If snapping a padlock shut requires that a small bar slips out of the way, shimming focuses on getting that bar out of the way. This is similar to the classic "credit card" attack, in which a credit card is used to slip back the latch of a locked door.

The photo below shows a traditional Master® brand combination lock after having been shimmed. The shim is slipped down the shackle into the chamber coming between the retaining bar and the notch on the shackle. This action pops open the lock.

Photos courtesy of Deviant

There are a few ways to determine if a lock can be shimmed. One of the easiest ways is to open the lock and prod the retaining bar (found inside the shackle chamber) with a small tool such as a pick or wrench tool. If the bar can be easily pushed out of the way, it is spring-loaded and can most likely be shimmed. If you're feeling like you've been drug into an uncharted wilderness of lockpicking technology and left for dead, let me try to put this a bit more simply: you can poke at a locks sensitive bits with a skinny stick to see if it can be opened with the same skinny stick. That's not too much of an over-generalization.

Some locks have notches on either side of the shackle, like the one shown in the next photo. This lock can be easily probed and shimmed, because despite the two notches, the lock has a single rudimentary retaining bar mechanism meant to accommodate the lock body no matter which way the body is affixed when the lock is secured.

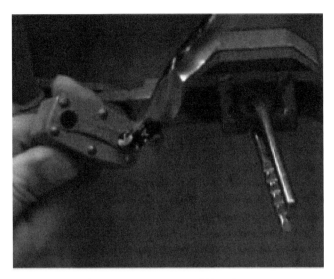

Photos courtesy of Deviant

If a multi-notched lock contains two separate retaining bars, shimming might become more difficult. Because of the way padlocks are constructed, it's not feasible to give the more hidden of these two bars the "poke test." But testing one bar is sufficient; if one side of a lock's retaining mechanism is spring-loaded, the other probably is as well. The problem with shimming a multi-notched lock is that you must use two shims, one for each notch. That can cause problems if the gaps along the shackle are tight. Store-bought shims made of spring steel tend to be too thick for this task, meaning that the attacker has to use something thinner, like a strip of aluminum from a soda or beer can. Think that's still too-much technical mumbo-jumbo? Remember, we're now talking about popping locks with *two* long skinny sticks. Generally.

Can I get you something? Beer, soda?

What is it with hackers and beer cans? Yes, it's possible to make a really decent shim out of an aluminum can. It's decidedly low-tech, and really works great, but in the interest of keeping this book from becoming a guide for criminals, I'll just float you a URL for Deviant's great overview: www.i-hacked.com/index.php?option=content&task=view&id=189.

Be sure to test your locks against this technique. It can be really hard for an amateur to determine if a lock is shimmable. The lock in the next photo, for example, is a Master lock that is readily available in most retail outlets. That often means you get what you pay for, but it features a double-ball mechanism and is not shimmable.

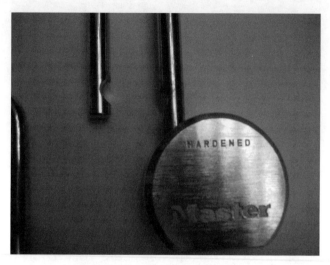

Photos courtesy of Deviant

Here are some tips to picking (no pun intended) a shim-proof lock:

1. A lock that can be *shut* without any key or combination is almost always spring-loaded internally and therefore susceptible to shimming.
2. A lock in which an operating key is permanently fixed during use (known as a *key retaining padlock*) will often not be susceptible to shimming.
3. Locks that advertise a "double ball" mechanism on their packaging can most likely not be shimmed.
4. Padlocks that feature a *collar* or *boot* on the shackle (the primary purpose of which is to frustrate the use of bolt cutters) are often difficult or impossible to shim. In addition to being hard to shim, such locks typically consist of higher quality construction and have a locking mechanism that provides better security.
5. Locksmiths will often recommend certain brands of padlocks. Trust their advice. Deviant recommends 8088 and 8077 series locks from Sargent & Greenleaf, which are used on Department of Defense filing cabinets. That's a double seal of approval.

Master Lock Combo Lock Brute Forcing

As a kid, I remember seeing the cool Master Lock commercial with the lock that was secure even after being drilled clean through by a rifle round. For me, Master® became synonymous with security. To this day, many people purchase Master Lock based on the brand name alone. However, do not buy just based on the brand name, because almost all brands offer locks at a variety of security levels. Always investigate all the product offerings to make sure you're getting a product that suits your needs. For example, this Master Lock model 1500D combination lock is sold everywhere.

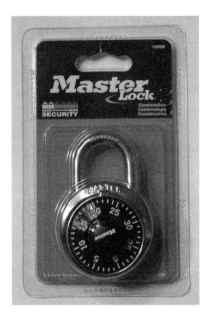

But the company does not promote this as a high-security lock. They recommend this lock be used for the most basic of security applications. Still, I see this exact lock used in high-security applications almost daily, despite the fact that there's a dangerous brute-force attack that renders most versions of this lock all but useless.

Brute forcing describes a technique in which every possible solution for a problem is checked to see if it is the solution. For example, on a barrel lock with three barrels, all possible combinations fall between 000 and 999. If someone started with 001, 002, 003, and progressively tried every possible combination, brute force guarantees they will open the lock in one thousand tries. Most mechanical combination locks can be brute-forced if an adversary has enough patience to complete the attack—and that's what gives a lock its level of security.

Fortunately most bad guys aren't patient enough to brute force a combination lock. In the case of the Master Lock, if we assume each of the numbers on the dial is active (which is not the case) we are left with 40^3 or 64,000 possible combinations. If an attacker tries one combination every five seconds—a reasonable speed considering the clearing process and the left-right turns—it could take as long as 88 hours, or nearly four days, to work through every combination. At this rate, the attacker would fail, not the lock.

A shortcut I'm about to describe to you reduces the number of combinations to 100. At five seconds per attempt, it would take an attacker a mere eight minutes to brute force one hundred combinations. Since this book is about protecting your own assets, I won't go into all the details required to open a lock using this technique, but I will tell you how to figure out the last number of your combination. If you can discover the third digit of your combination, you should get a stronger lock. Better yet, have a professional locksmith evaluate your situation.

To begin, apply tension to the shackle of the lock. A simple way to do this is to hold the lock in one hand and use a finger to apply upward pressure on the shaft, as shown in the next photo. The stylish thumb ring is optional for this exercise.

Next, begin turning the dial. If enough tension is applied, the dial should stick between two numbers. I'll call this a *sticking point*. Twelve sticking points exist on each affected lock. The first step is to find and record the location of each sticking point. For example, the lower boundary of this lock's first sticking point is, as shown in the next photo.

The high boundary of this same sticking point is 2, as shown in this next photo.

This midpoint between these digits is 1.5, which is obviously not a whole number. To find the next sticking point, release the tension on the shackle, turn the dial past the current sticking point's high boundary and reapply tension. The dial should stick again, revealing the location of the next sticking point. Some sticking points will rest on whole numbers. For example, the next photo shows that the low boundary of the next sticking point is 7.5.

I realize that you, kind reader understand what I'm talking about without all these pictures, but let's just take a look at one more so that we've covered even, odd, high and low sticking points. The high boundary of this same sticking point is 8.5 as shown in the next photo.

This means that the sticking point rests on. By keeping a record of each sticking point, you will eventually arrive at something like what I've got in this table.

The Sticking Points on My Lock

Low Boundary	High Boundary	Sticking Point
1	2	1.5
4	5	4.5
7.5	8.5	8
11	12	11.5
14.5	15.5	15
17.5	18.5	18
21	22	21.5
24	25	24.5
27.5	28.5	28
31	32	31.5
34	35	34.5
37.5	38.5	38

Notice that more than half of the sticking points do not land on whole numbers. These are decoys and should be removed from the list of potential combination digits. In this example, that leaves five numbers: 8, 15, 18, 28, and 38. Notice that most of these numbers end in the same digit—the number eight. These matching numbers should be removed from the list as well, leaving only one number (15) which is the last digit of my lock's combination.

If this technique works on your lock, there's a good chance the lock is vulnerable to a brute force attack. If the technique does not work, you may have a newer 1500D Master Lock. It is speculated (on www.wikihow.com/Crack-a-Master-Combination-Lock) that 1500D Master Locks with serial numbers beginning with the number 800 are not vulnerable to this attack, although unverified sources have reported success against these newer locks as well. Either way, don't be quick to throw stones at Master Lock. Do your research, and don't purchase basic security products for high security tasks. Consider purchasing a higher security Master Lock for your application, or get the advice of a professional locksmith or security professional.

Get Real!

Several Web sites discuss this vulnerability in great detail. However, there's a decent amount of math and memorization involved in determining the first and second digits of the combination. Tim "Thor" Mullen presents a shortcut he worked out in *Stealing the Network: How to Own a Shadow* by Syngress Publishing. The story, co-authored by Tim, Ryan "Blue Boar" Russell, and myself, tells a "gripping" tale of what hackers are capable of in the real world. By all accounts, the story is fiction, but the techniques, like the Master Lock brute force, are not. Check out the entire *Stealing* series to see what you might be up against when the hackers take the gloves off!

Toilet Paper vs. Tubular Locks

Tubular locks are used in all sorts of applications, but they are often found in laptop security devices, like the one shown in the next photo.

In 1992, the BBC reported that certain tubular locks were vulnerable to bypass by unskilled thieves. Twelve years later, in August of 2004, Marc Tobias, author of *Locks, Safes, and Security*[2] found that Kensington and Targus were using similar cylindrical axial designs in their laptop lock products. His report suggested that the locks could be easily bypassed with a pen or a toilet paper tube. In September of 2004, Chris Brennan described on his forums (www.bikeforums.net) how an expensive Kryptonite bike lock (which used the same cylindrical axial design) could be bypassed with a Bic pen. Chris posted videos to www.bikeforums.net/video and a media frenzy ensued.

Enter Barry Wels of Toool. While presenting at a hacker conference, Barry created a video (http://www.toool.nl/kensington623.wmv) showing how to apply the bypass technique to a specific Kensington laptop lock system. The hacker community found the video interesting, but the general public was awed by the fact that he accomplished the bypass in mere moments using the cardboard from a toilet paper roll.

[2] Ibid.

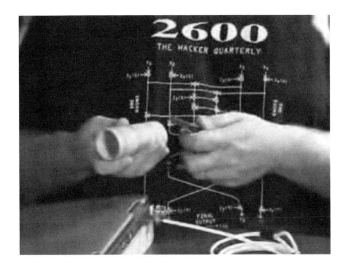

While there is always speculation about who thought of what first, nearly a million people have downloaded the video from Barry's site, and countless others have downloaded it from sites like You Tube.com. I love Barry's video because it is so accessible and it clearly demonstrates what I'm trying to show in this book even the most complex security systems are at risk from simple attacks. If you have sensitive data on a laptop, and you rely on a single locking device to protect that data, you'll probably get burned whether or not the lock is vulnerable to this attack. Whenever you rely on a single layer of security, odds are you'll be compromised. A laptop lock isn't a bad idea, but if you're concerned about losing sensitive data on the machine, consider some sort of crypto solution as well. Above all, try to think like a hacker. In that frame of mind, is a spindly cable the best solution?

Electric Flossers: A Low-Tech Classic

Lock picking takes real skill. To do it right, you've got to have a working knowledge of how locks operate and you need to practice. With the advent of newer devices such as lock picking guns and other electric tools lock picking seems more accessible than ever. Still, these tools are not foolproof. They require a decent amount of skill to successfully operate. In addition, they are expensive. Most amateurs would not consider investing a small fortune in a specialized device that's not foolproof.

Still, there's a certain allure to gadget hacking, and the lock picking community had a field day with new-fangled electric flossing devices, like this one.

I'm not sure who came up with the idea of hacking this innocent-looking thing, but someone did. The result was a tiny, inexpensive electric lock-picking gun. According to Jared Bouck over at Inventgeek.com, this little device, when combined with even a makeshift tension wrench, will open most padlocks in a matter of seconds.

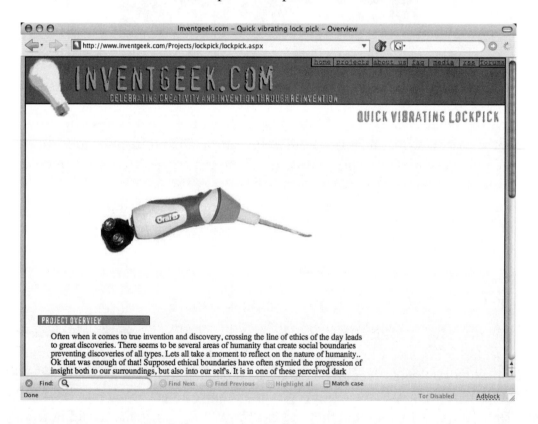

This hack involves modifying the flosser to accept a stronger power source. Then the flosser, when inserted into a lock, can vibrate hard enough to jiggle tumblers out of the locked position. Be sure to check out www.inventgeek.com for more information, and be sure to full-body tackle anyone you see skulking around with an electric flosser. They're definitely up to something.

Laptop Locks Defeated by Beer
(*With Matt Fiddler and Marc Weber Tobias*)

Many combination locks are vulnerable to an attack known as "probing the gates." In this technique a small shim is used to probe the combination wheels of the lock (shown in the next photo) in an attempt to locate "gates," or openings, which will reveal the combination and ultimately open the lock. In August 2004, Security.org reported that the Targus Defcon CL "Computer Cable Lock" (model number PA410U) was vulnerable to this method of attack.

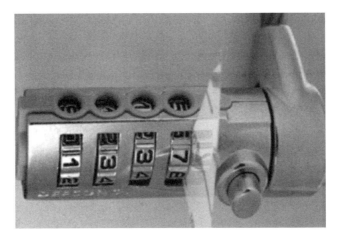

Photo courtesy of Marc Weber Tobias

As a result, Targus re-engineered their lock to remedy this exposure. The new incarnation of the lock (the Defcon "Armored" CL, model number ASP10US) sported a new armored cable. Analysis verified that Targus had remedied the initial problem by moving the gates to the interior of the lock cylinders. However, a new method was discovered that exposed the lock to probing through the combination change screw at the end of the lock body. This technique would allow an attacker to probe the gates (one cylinder at a time), but in order to pull off this attack, a bag guy would either need to remove the plastic cover, or slip a very thin shim past the cover.

Photo courtesy of Marc Weber Tobias

Enter the beer can. This attack requires a shim .015" or less in thickness. Physical security experts Matt Fiddler and Marc Weber Tobias found that a strip cut from a beer can, measuring only .005" thick, works perfectly.

Photo courtesy of Marc Weber Tobias

But the abuse of this lock continued, and Mike and Marc revealed that the cable itself could be attacked. In order to do so, a bad guy would first need to remove the thin plastic coating from the cable. As shown in the next photo, a cigarette lighter makes quick work of the thin PVC coating.

Photo courtesy of Marc Weber Tobias

With the PVC cover removed, the lock could be pinched and cut using nothing more than a standard pair of diagonal wire cutters, as shown in the next photo.

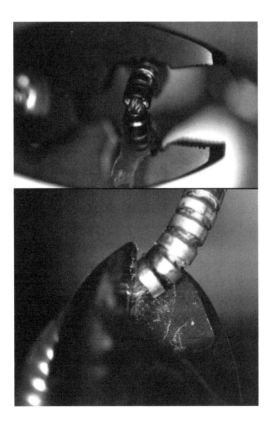

As these tests reveal, it pays to be vigilant when selecting any security device, but laptop locks are especially critical. The data on a laptop is often worth more than the hardware itself. Invest wisely and test properly. It always pays to do research on any security device before using it.

TSA Locks (*With Marc Weber Tobias*)

Because of the increased airline security measures following 9/11, the Transportation and Safety Administration (TSA) prohibited the use of standard locks on luggage. However, they do allow "TSA locks" which can be locked by a passenger and opened and relocked by a TSA agent without disturbing the combination set by the passenger. These locks, shown below, have become a common site at airline baggage terminals all over the world.

All photos in this section provided courtesy of Marc Weber Tobias

Marc Weber Tobias performed an audit of each of these locks, publishing the results in a paper entitled "TSA-Approved Luggage Locks" (http://download.security.org/ tsa_luggage_locks_report.pdf). His summary is a no-tech hacker's dream come true, outlining the weaknesses in the locks themselves, but also pointing out that most locked luggage is simple to break into without fiddling with the lock:

Each of the mechanisms that were examined in this report can be easily bypassed without any special tools or expertise, often in a few seconds. Passengers should not rely on these locks to provide any security. Although baggage handling specialists point out that luggage can be easily opened by cutting outer material or circumventing the zipper, the real issue in the view of the author is the introduction of contraband by a third party, or a delayed detection of the theft of contents. This report examines each type of lock and its vulnerability to surreptitious entry.

Marc discovered that many of the locks could be opened with rudimentary strips of metal or plastic like the ones shown below.

His paper went on to describe how gate-probing techniques (like those used to open the DEFCON CL series locks) could be used on each of the TSA locks as well. Armed with a bit of plastic like the one shown below, an adversary could determine the lock's combination, one wheel and one value at a time.

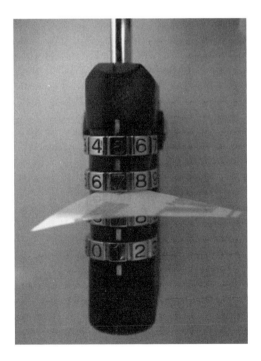

In some cases, an adversary may be required to perform a bit of simple addition or subtraction to determine the true combination of the lock, but we're talking second grade arithmetic here, not algebra.

Ross Kinard, an IT professional associated with SploitCast, is no fan of TSA locks:

Because [TSA locks] are mostly "sesame" locks, most inherit the problems [of other "sesame" locks]. Those that are not "sesame" locks can be taken apart to learn what the key depths are for the master keys. From my experience, the 002 can be opened using just about any piece of metal you can fit in the keyway and jiggle, while the key that comes with the […] can be filed down to work on [other 001 locks]. The 004 just needs a small strong piece of metal to turn [the inside cam], and the key that comes with the 007 works on all other 007s.

Marc's final judgment is damning indeed:

It is clear that none of the TSA-approved locks provide any measure of security against covert entry. The question for the user must be "what security is required to protect my luggage from pilfering?" The answer clearly involves more than just locks, and perhaps luggage can never really be secured[…].

The conclusion of this report is quite simple: do not rely upon these locks for any level of security. They are simply a form of expensive seal that can be reset. A knowledgeable individual can open any of these locks by decoding the combination, with very limited training or expertise. And, one can purchase these locks anywhere, so practice before theft is not a problem. Use of a key, of course, makes the task quite simple, and would allow virtually anyone that has contact with a piece of luggage the ability to open it.

Our advice compliments what the experts are saying: consider the contents of your check-in luggage to be public property to anyone sufficiently motivated, airport employee or not. Carry what you can't afford to lose, and remain suspicious of your bags after they have been out of your site for any length of time.

Gun Trigger Locks vs. Drinking Straw (*With Marc Tobias and Matt Fiddler*)

When I sat down to consider the list of physical no-tech hacks I would include in this book, I never considered covering an attack against gun trigger locks. The simple fact is that I rarely run into them in my line of work. But because of Marc Tobias and Matt Fiddler's excellent reputation, I flipped through their "Report on Gun Locks," available from http://download.security.org/gunlock_2007.pdf. I was amazed to find a very deadly no-tech hack, which I vaguely outline here. Although I don't think it would be responsible to fully describe the bypass technique here, I feel it's necessary to help Marc and Matt get the word out about the danger of the inferior locking systems they cover in their report. If you have any of the locks described in this section, replace them immediately with more secure models.

The most ridiculous attack centers on the DAC trigger-lock (shown below) which can be found in major retail chains including Wal-Mart and K-Mart.

This lock consists of a typical clam shell design which shrouds the gun's trigger and guard. The halves are secured by a threaded bolt that mates to a provided key. In the locked position the head of the bolt is recessed into the lock's body. Marc and Matt discovered that a McDonald's drinking straw could be used to open the lock with relative ease, as shown in the next two photos.

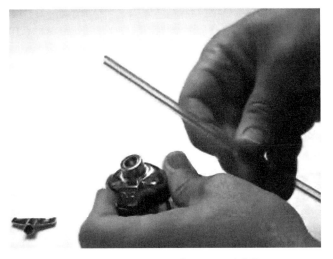

Photos courtesy of Matt Fiddler

Ross Kinard adds that the key that comes with this lock can be filed in such a way that it will open all other DAC brand gun locks. The report goes on to say that many other brands of gun lock are vulnerable to compromise as well, including certain Master Lock, Remington and Winner International locks, some of which can be opened by a child with an ice pick or sharp screwdriver. In fact, Marc reports that each and every one of the trigger locks shown below contains a serious vulnerability. These include, but are not limited to the U.S. Department of Justice "Project Childsafe" gun cable lock; the Master Lock Trigger Lock Models 90, 94 and 106; the DAC MTL 100 Trigger Lock; the Franzen Combination Lock; the GSM Gun Trigger Lock and the Winchester Gun Case.

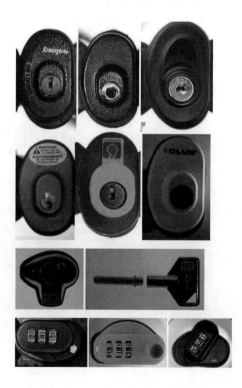

The U.S. Consumer Product Safety Commission maintains a list of recalled products on its website at http://www.cpsc.gov. Many responsible vendors such as Master Lock have issued recalls on their products; for instance, certain versions of the Model 90 shown below. You should search the cpsc.gov website for your locks to make sure they haven't been recalled. I hereby refrain from making any sort of smart-alec comment about gun locks. This is *way* too serious of a topic.

Gun Safety

If you have guns, they should be locked with quality trigger locks, and stored inside a locked cabinet. Practice responsible key control, and remain vigilant about the security of your firearms. Most importantly, have your security arrangement evaluated by a professional locksmith.

Entry Techniques: Loiding (*aka the Old Credit Card Trick*)

It seems like everyone knows about the credit card trick. In fact, it's the one entry technique an average person can pull off without training, given the right circumstances. Still, I seem to run into the right circumstances all the time because I get this working a little too often. The technical term for this technique is *loiding*. The way it works is simple. To get past a locked window, an attacker may try to slip a credit card (or a thin, strong bit of wire) between the window stiles in order to throw the latch into the unlocked position. To get past a door, the attacker will slip the card between the door strike and the latch bolt in an attempt to separate the bolt from the door strike, which will open the door (assuming there's only one engaged lock on the door).

There must be a gap between the door panel and the doorjamb in order for this technique to work. The photo below shows an exaggerated gap.

OK, so that's more of a door *chasm*, and it wouldn't take much to get a finger in there, if it weren't for that clever security device (the steel plate) covering it. The plate does solve the credit card problem, but as you can see from the next photo (shot looking down inside the door gap at the latch mechanism) the gap is so ginormous that another type of tool could be used to bypass the door.

A no-tech hacker wouldn't be daunted by this misplaced security measure. One look at the surrounding area reveals the trash can shown in the next photo.

After making sure there are no interesting documents in the trash, a no-tech hacker would most likely grab the small length of network cable. As shown in the photo below, it fits perfectly into the door gap.

With a simple tug, the door opens, as shown below.

I'm constantly amazed at how often this technique works. I've used it more times than I can count, and clients are rarely happy to hear that their security systems have been bested by a bit of garbage. Keep an eye out for this vulnerability in the security systems you care about. Now, I know this chapter is longer than many of the others, but physical security is about more than just locks. In this next section, we'll take a look at other physical security devices often abused by no-tech hackers. So grab some coffee and try not to cringe in abject fear of every door or lock you walk past on the way to the coffee machine. We've got more ground to cover.

Entry Techniques: Motion Sensor Activation

Try really hard to ignore the words *motion sensor* in this section's header. Got it out of your mind? Now, with a clear perspective, check out the locked entrance in the photo below. What are the options for a no-tech attack?

Photo courtesy of Russell Handorf

Well, first there's a card reader mounted on the wall. A technical attacker might think of cloning a card or breaking out the tools to disassemble that thing. I'll give props to anyone stone-cold elite enough to bypass this thing with alligator clips and a screwdriver. But that's not the attack we're interested in.

The next thing to check out might be the tolerances between the door and the frame. The tolerances are tight, and despite the fact that the door latch is clearly visible, the lock is not susceptible to loiding. A softer option may be to social engineer an employee in some way. Tailgating comes to mind as well, but either of these softer options might tip off an employee that something's not quite right, even if the attack succeeds initially. The best option is to wait and watch. Inevitably, an employee will exit, and a no-tech hacker will get a glimpse of the exit procedure in use.

As I mentioned in the Introduction, Vince taught me that it's often easier to get out of a building than it is to get in. I've leveraged this simple fact every single time I've broken into one of my client's secured buildings. And in this case, that advice pays off after waiting a few moments. An employee exits through the door with a jarring *shi-clack*. Since the employee didn't swipe a badge or grab the door handle to exit, the question becomes: How did that process work? A glimpse through the window at the inside of the door reveals little. There's no push bar to be seen, and no evidence of any sort of latch or button. The handle on the inside of the door is exactly the same as the one on the outside. The answer lie not in what is *seen* but what is *heard*, and specifically *when* it was heard.

That sound was the distinctively loud clack of a magnetic lock disengaging. There are quite a few techniques for disabling a magnetic lock, but it's not the target of this particular attack. The target is the motion sensor that disengaged the magnetic lock. Both are shown in this next photo, taken from inside the locked area.

Photo courtesy of Russell Handorf

The existence of the motion sensor is obvious to a no-tech hacker for two reasons: the door disengaged before the employee reached the door, and as seen through the window, the employee made no specific motion to unlock the door. The motion sensor did all the work. Allowing employees to exit the area without a special key or procedure is more than mere convenience. In a fire, this setup can save lives.

A skilled no-tech hacker can bypass this system simply, and in any number of ways. In homage to Vince, we elect to use the junk shown in the next photo.

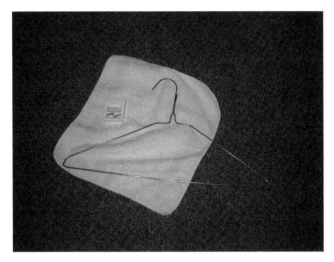

Photo courtesy of Russell Handorf

Attaching the washcloth to the straightened hanger with a bit of dental floss, a no-tech attacker can make a flag which can be slipped under the door and waved. It eventually trips the motion sensor, which unlocks this door. Test your exit procedures. Your way out may be an adversary's best way in.

Defeating Motion Sensors with Toys?

Sure thing. A simple sheet of white paper may be enough to trip up these sensors if you can slip it in above the door and let it flutter past the sensor. A paper airplane is much more fun. Fold it flat, slip it through the crack and let it fly. Even balloons—the long twisty kind used to make balloon animals—make great no-tech tools. Simply slip one under the door, inflate it and start waving it around. Just make sure you let everyone know you're testing the security system ahead of time. Getting whacked in the head with a door is no fun.

Bypassing Passive Infrared (PIR) Motion Sensors

Passive Infrared (PIR) motion sensors are used in many complex alarm systems, but basic systems are fairly easy to bypass. You can not see passive infrared fields because they do not emit infrared light (see the sidebar). Rather, they detect infrared energy such as that radiated from humans, or at least humans who are warmer than 93° Fahrenheit.

Seeing Infrared Light

If you ever need to detect infrared light, try using a digital camera's viewfinder. This photo shows the normally invisible infrared light emitted from a TV remote control as seen through a digital camera's viewfinder.

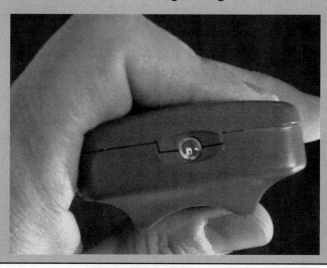

These types of sensors *sudden* changes in the infrared field it monitors, which means they can be bypassed by easing into and through their monitoring field. Ross Kinard sent me this photo of an entrance, monitored by a PIR sensor mounted above the left-hand doorway.

Photo courtesy of Ross Kinard

Ross maps out his successful bypass of the sensor system in the diagram below.

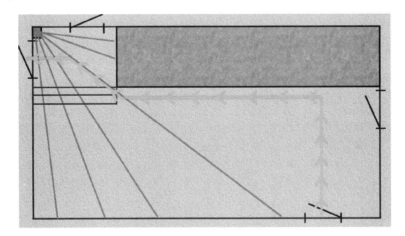

Photo courtesy of Ross Kinard

Since the sensor had been set up to cover the two doors in the upper left corner of the diagram, it was blind to his entrance through the door in the opposite corner. He made his way to the opposite wall and traversed along it, staying out of the sensor's field for most of his approach. Reaching the edge of the field, he played it smart and turned directly into the IR beam. By doing this, he was able to maintain the ever-so-peppy pace of one foot every four to twelve seconds. According to Ross, "That part was pretty easy. The tough part was moving across to the door. Then I moved really slow, about two to four inches at a time with about a six second interval between each move. This is where I kept messing up. I didn't realize how slow I needed to go, but I eventually got it."

In one of my favorite films, *Sneakers* (1992), Martin Bishop (Robert Redford) dressed in a neoprene suit in order to take on a motion sensor. His cohort (River Phoenix) prepared the room in advance by raising the room's temperature to match Bishop's body temperature. In painfully slow steps, Bishop reached his goal without tripping the alarm. According to the crew of the awesome show *MythBusters,* many elements of this scene ring true. In the second part of *Crimes and Myth-Demeanors* (http://shopping.discovery.com/index.html), the Mythbusters – Kari, Grant and Tory – took on several security devices including PIR and ultrasonic motion sensors. They found that the "slow and low" technique also works well against ultrasonic sensors, which use high-frequency sound instead of infrared light. They also discovered that a neoprene suit would hide an intruder's heat signature from a PIR sensor for a short while. But eventually, the suit absorbs the intruder's body heat, making him visible to the sensor again. They also tried raising the room's temperature to 98°F in order to fool a PIR sensor, but this test failed—the sensor triggered immediately. They were able to bypass a PIR sensor by placing a piece of glass in front of the sensor, but this would only work if the temperature of the glass was close enough to the temperature of the room. In the most surprising test, Kari spread a bed sheet in front of herself while crossing an ultrasonic field and the alarm was not triggered.

IR Sensors Hacked In Major Heist

In one major heist, chronicled at www.crimelibrary.com/gangsters_outlaws/outlaws/major_heists/2.html, a smart thief sprayed silicone spray over the IR sensors during business hours. This effectively blinded the sensors, which could not detect heat changes beyond the silicone coating.

Camera Flaring

Surveillance cameras are one of the most common physical security devices I've run into. But many camera installations are so poorly configured that an amateur can bypass them without much effort. *Flaring* is simply blinding or overloading a camera so that it can't record anything meaningful. Amateur thieves have known about this technique for years, but I'm amazed to find that it still works against many modern systems. Russell Handorf, a CISSP working out of the Philadelphia area, provided this next photo of a typical camera installation.

Photo courtesy of Russell Handorf

The first thing a no-tech hacker might notice is that the camera's data and power cables are exposed. In this particular installation, however, the cables are armored, making them difficult to sever. Also, the cable connectors to the back of the cameras are locked, making them toughcult to remove. The cameras themselves are very high-end: Topica (Sony chipset) model TP-936WIR-30C, equipped with 20-LED infrared night vision.

A typical still image captured from this system is shown below.

Photo courtesy of Russell Handorf

So what's the no-tech hack? We call it camera *flaring*, and it's nothing more than simply blinding the camera with an extremely bright light. In this next photo, Russ flares the light with a SureFire x300 LED light. As you can see (or not see) the camera is completely blinded by a direct hit from this extremely bright light.

Photo courtesy of Russell Handorf

This technique offers the attacker room for error. An indirect hit from a SureFire or a direct hit with a weaker light will produce a decent effect, as the next photo shows.

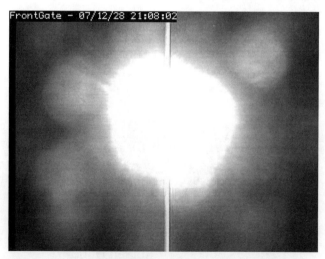

Photo courtesy of Russell Handorf

Other light sources can do the trick as well, even from quite a distance away. Take a look at the next image capture. This is my "arrest me" face.

A quick swipe with a cheap laser pointer makes it difficult to make out my face, as the next capture shows.

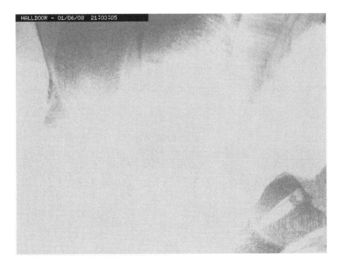

The next capture shows the effect of a direct hit on the lens. As you can see, it's impossible to make out anything in the image—the camera is completely blinded.

Your surveillance systems are vulnerable to these attacks, you might consider using better equipment, installing additional cameras to cover multiple angles, or consider installing a filter or reflective dome to protect your camera lens. Remember though that anything placed in front of the lens will affect the image quality. Be especially careful when using IR filters. They can block the light needed to illuminate the field at night, effectively destroying the camera's night-vision capability.

Real World: Airport Restricted Area Simplex Lock Bypass

Simplex locks (such as the one shown below) have a wicked reputation.

Noted security researcher Michal Zalewski goes high-tech against locks like this and his results are nothing short of spectacular. In his paper "Cracking Safes With Thermal Imaging" (http://lcamtuf.coredump.cx/tsafe), Michal shows that heat left behind from a user's fingerprints can be detected with a thermal imaging device up to several minutes later, as shown below.

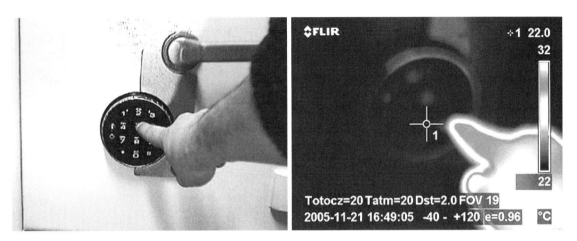

Popular video games like *Splinter Cell* have gotten in on this action, too. The in-game photo below shows a combo lock as seen through Sam Fisher's thermal goggles moments after a guard punched in the combo.

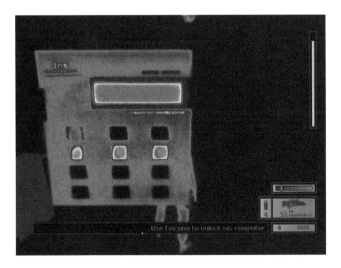

In my opinion Michal's truth is cooler than video game fiction, but either way, thermal imaging is a pretty sweet high-tech attack. But this book is about no-tech, so let's get to the no-tech options. Since the buttons used most often will have a thin layer of finger-oil residue, you could dust the panel with baby powder, and blow away the excess to find the combo buttons. Or you can trick a user who knows the combo into touching some UV-reactive gunk so that when he or she touches the buttons you can later hit the panel with a UV light to see which buttons were touched, sort of like that scene in *National Treasure*. You could even brute-force these puppies if you've got serious hand-eye coordination and aren't prone to bouts of carpel tunnel.

But so far, the techniques I've discussed are not truly no-tech. These attacks require actual tools and some gear, and at the very least some baby powder. Let's go all the way down to no-tech for a real-world attack. Come with me as I head to the airport, home of some of the most paranoid and advanced security systems anywhere, armed only with my eyeballs and an optional digital camera in search of a prime shoulder surfing opportunity.

Past the security screening checkpoints, I spot several Simplex locks, but they all have the distinct look of a janitor's closet. Eventually, though, I find a Simplex lock protecting what appears to be an office door. The door is adjacent to a gate checking area, and as I step closer a pilot walks up to the door, punches the digits and pushes through, revealing a windowed office overlooking the runway, and a computer system. Thrilled to see that the lock protects an actual office, but bummed that I missed the combo, I look for a good place to sit and wait for another pilot to poke out the digits. The perfect seat would be relatively close to the door and at an angle that allows me to see the buttons clearly as they are entered. I find the perfect seat, and just as I am about to sit down, I spot this sign:

I dutifully ignore the sign, plop down in the "restricted area," and pull out my laptop. I set my camera on the keyboard, making sure that it's out of view of casual passers by, and wait. I do have to wait long. Within moments, a pilot comes by and punches out the combination. The stills below speak for themselves.

Although I've presented the stills in a random order (and maybe even removed one or two) the message is still clear: shoulder surfing rules, especially when you left your thermal imager in your other pants. The pilot pushes through the door, leaving it wide open. I lift my camera and continue filming. The next shot shows shoulder surfing, Round Two.

I purposely blurred the image to protect the innocent, but even still, do you see what I see? I hope you do because that means this book is teaching you something. I know you can't read anything in the photo, but you should be able to pinpoint at least five items a no-tech hacker would focus on for more information. Do you see them? Go ahead, give it a try before you continue reading.

How did you do? The monitor is a gimme. We've got a whole chapter on shoulder surfing monitors. What about the stickies *on* the monitor—one small, and one super-sized? One could be a barcode, and the other could be just about anything. Let's go deeper. What about the brand of monitor? Combined with the barcode, it may give you a clue about who handles tech support at the airport. Social engineering, anyone? What about the laser printer? Again we see another sticky that may list instructions for the printer, IP addresses, print queue names and more. The brand of printer might clue us in to another social engineering gag. We could be the printer repair guy. There's other stuff here as well. Did you catch the seriously old and discolored dot-matrix printer? It's got stickies, too—more than one. Check out the sign above the phone. Could it have important extensions? Did you catch the poster? Could it contain industry jargon important for a social engineering attack? The pilot at the terminal can be visually disassembled as well, even though we could just as easily do this outside the office. Is he married or single? Ex-military or civilian? Neat or messy? The list could go on and on.

The next photo sums up the success of this real-world scenario, as I capture not only a shoulder surfing session and a roomful of potential information, but also one pilot's lanyard and string of badges. So many options in one photo.

The point here is not to pick on the airport's security, or the pilot's lack of awareness, or the TSA's obliviousness to the whole affair. Rather, the point is that even in an environment where security is a top priority, no-tech hackers can have an absolute field day. If it's possible to gather all this information in mere moments at an airport, it's possible anywhere.

Chapter 5

Social Engineering: Here's How I Broke Into Their Buildings

Social engineering is the most essential weapon in a no-tech hacker's arsenal, but as a society, we have a love/hate relationship with those that excel at the art. We dig "social engineer good guys" like Zorro, Clark Kent, and the Scarlet Pimpernel; we hate others like Robert Hanssen (subject of the movie "Breach"), Aldrich Ames or that cheating

Significant Other. Whatever your thoughts about social engineers, you should at least understand the mindset, and learn what you can do to protect yourself and those around you, because social engineers have one huge advantage: they're playing you before you even realize there's a game to be played.

Introduction

By this point you've probably noticed that a no-tech hacker is equal parts opportunist, actor, and con artist. Security experts roll up all of that and more in the term *social engineer*. A hacker experiments with a piece of technology to see if he can get useful results from it that its creator never intended. A social engineer does the same thing with human relationships.

The first part of this chapter is written by Jack Wiles. Jack is a security professional with over thirty years of experience in computer security, cyber-crime prevention, disaster recovery and physical security. He has trained hundreds of federal agents, corporate attorneys, CEOs and internal auditors on computer crime and security-related topics. His unforgettable presentations are filled with three decades of personal "war stories" from the trenches of Information Security and Physical Security. Because social engineering is at the heart of no-tech hacking, and Jack knows social engineering, I'm putting you in his capable hands. Take it, Jack!

How Easy Is It?

As an inside penetration team leader, I learned every exploit I could to conduct a successful inside penetration test. It was during those years that I gained most of my social engineering experience. These skills helped me to eventually hang up my dumpster diving penetration team jersey and retire from the Tiger Team world *undefeated*. Although I had several close calls, I was never stopped or reported to security as a possible burglar or corporate espionage agent, even though that's the role I was playing—effectively, it's what I was.

In 1988 I was part of an internal security team for a large corporation. On several occasions, I had the opportunity to hear conversations that went on when a "black hat" (or malicious) group targeted a victim by calling on the phone. The black hats were using social engineering skills to gain access to proprietary information, including passwords. What I heard one of the veteran black hats say to a trainee remains true today: "Social engineering is the easiest way to break into a system."

Why do attackers prefer social engineering as their attack vector? Let's say you are an elite black hat hacker, and an international conglomerate has offered you big money if you can provide them valid sign-in credentials for their chief rival's corporate network. In short, they want one or more user names and passwords.

Let's call the target company International Acronym. As a "leet" black hat, you see no challenge whatsoever in learning user names for Acronym's network. Most big corporations assign user names systematically, derived from employee names. If Joe Doaks works for Acronym, his user name is probably one of a few variations: joedoaks, jdoaks, JDoaks@Acronym, or some equivalent. If you can learn employee names, you can figure out user names. One obvious way to do this is to snag a printed corporate phone book (more on this later). But since you're a smart and competent high-tech attacker, instead, you search Acronym's Web site and find some names. You have many to choose from: executives, a PR person, a tech support manager, a marketing drone quoted in an interview… an email address here and there indicate what the structure of user names probably is. Great! All you need now is a password.

I'm about to compare what a high-tech hacker does to obtain a targeted valid password, versus what a no-tech hacker does to get a password. Ready? Here are the high-tech steps:

- *Scan Acronym's network* to see if any ports are listening on the Internet. You could scan the whole range of 65,000 ports in a matter of seconds, but Acronym's Intrusion Detection Systems would go off like a Christmas tree wearing a car alarm. You're too smart for that, so you perform your scan in stealth mode. You have to go in low and slow, scanning one port every few seconds, ideally from IP addresses all over the huge botnet you control.

- *Install malware on a victim machine.* Assuming your port scan successfully reveals an open port, you next want to sneak your rootkit onto Acronym's network. You program a little script that can exploit a dozen recently patched vulnerabilities, in hopes that Acronym hasn't kept up with patching every application on their network. Packing and crypting a chunk of code that exploits holes in Internet Explorer, Quicktime, Yahoo's toolbar, WinAmp, and other popular apps, you send it off. Like making your first million dollars, getting that first victim is the hardest. But since you're so "leet," we'll stipulate that you successfully land your code on one of Acronym's networked computers.

- *Enumerate the target network.* Congrats! You're on Acronym's network. But how large is it? How many subnets does it have? Does it use routers, or switches? What connects to what? Can you find servers that contain password files? You'll have to carefully map out the network, hiding your activity the whole time. And in today's dog-eat-dog network environment, you might also have to fight off other hackers, or at least seal the security hole that got you in—so that a less careful hacker doesn't blunder in and blow your cover.

- *Locate and copy the encrypted password file.* Let's assume Acronym runs a Windows network. You'll probably use a tool like *pwdump* to snag a usable copy of their password hashes that you can ship to your own network to try to get at all those valuable passwords in clear text. You must move from one Acronym computer to another, like a series of stepping stones, moving ever closer to the main password server. And of course, you must do all this while concealing your activities, modifying logs and altering registry keys so that certain files do not update the date they were accessed.

- *Run automated cracking tools against the encrypted password file.* With the password hashes in your possession, and your activity on the Acronym network carefully hidden, you rev up John the Ripper loaded with all your favorite dictionaries and a huge rainbow table. Once this process begins, you'll probably have a few passwords in less than an hour. (If you'd like to see this working under lab conditions, check out the SecurityWise video, "How Password Crackers Work," found at http://video.google.com/videoplay?docid=4683570944129697667).

Whew! That was uber-leet, but you pulled it off. And it only took about a week. Now let's go for the same goal – a valid password on Acronym's network – the no-tech way. Ready? Count the steps:

- Make a phone call.

- Make another phone call. While you're chatting, ask for—and receive—valid login credentials.

Badda-bing, badda-done. In a moment, I'll show you how that's possible. For now, line up those two procedures side by side, and you can see why hackers find social engineering easier than high-tech attacks.

And the two-step version is the *difficult* version. Sometimes the Social Engineering Gods drop nuggets right into your lap. I stood on a street corner in Seattle waiting for a bus one day, and I overheard two workers near me discussing their corporate network. One employee described to the other his cool new password, stating it out in the open. He probably assumed this was safe because he felt anonymous. But when I took an incredulous glance back to see what kind of reckless wild man blabs his password on a street corner, there, dangling from a pocket of his cargo pants, was his employee identity badge. There was his name. Right above the logo for Amazon.com, whose headquarters was two buildings away. Amazing.

Social engineering can be that easy.

Even better: social engineering doesn't rely on a faulty piece of high-tech equipment to mount the attack. Rather, it uses a skilled attack on the psyche of the opponent. Most of the time, it can be accomplished with a clipboard and a cheap business card. So besides being easy, social engineering can be dirt cheap. (Even crooks worry about overhead cutting into their profit margin.)

Over the past fifteen years, I have learned first hand just how easy it is to be an effective con man as I lead several inside penetration teams into client's buildings who had hired us to test their vulnerabilities. Not one time did we fail or get caught as we roamed their buildings pretending to be employees. Everyone we encountered as we did our thing thought we belonged there.

How was that possible? Why, it's just human nature.

Human Nature, Human Weakness

This is certainly not the first written work discussing social engineering. The more you read the various articles and books on the topic, the more clearly the common thread begins to emerge. A social engineer turns our sympathetic, helpful human nature against us and exploits us with it.

One of the best books on the topic comes from Kevin Mitnick, widely regarded as the King of Social Engineers. His book *The Art of Deception: Controlling the Human Element of Security* demonstrates in story after story the exploitability of human kindness.

Mitnick would often pose as someone who was in trouble or had a problem which could be solved if he just had one little piece of information from the person he was talking with. Usually the information he requested wouldn't strike his target as sensitive data. For example, if you work at a bank branch in a national chain of banks, and someone calls asking for the address of another bank in the same chain, that doesn't seem like information you should withhold. So people answered his questions. In the conversation, they unwittingly leaked *more* information: Slang terms that only insiders used. The official name of a form. How many digits are in an account number.

Mitnick excelled at assembling these innocuous bits of data and leveraging them to get more data. If someone calls you and uses all the slangy insider terms of your business, seems conversant in numbering systems unique to your office, and even mirrors your feelings about management and customers, you're going to think that person is an "us," not a "them." And we always want to help "us."

I'm certainly not against kindness. But it should co-exist with wariness. For this discussion, let's consider threats from people who never were employees and don't belong in your building. That kind of stranger should be easy to spot, and easy to stop, right? Right?

Hello? Is this thing on?

"Strangers who don't belong in the building" is the category that my inside penetration team would fit into. When we roamed through buildings unchallenged, we definitely didn't belong there (other than being hired to try to get there, but none of the employees knew about that). Someone checking out your building for possible espionage or future terrorist activities would also fit in this category. In theory, some employee inside the building should eventually figure out that there is a Trojan horse in the camp. Someone has gotten past whatever security there is at the perimeter, where entry was gained. Yet that was never what we encountered.

When I spent years doing this for a living, we were hired expecting to get caught. Our attacks were designed to become increasingly bold the longer I had the team in a building. Toward the end of just about every job, we were openly walking around as if we worked there, almost hoping to get caught by someone. We never did! Employees, time after time, acted in gullible bliss.

C'mon. Kindness and a desire to help is one thing. Being a sucker is a whole 'nother thing. For more than three decades now, I have observed a lack of awareness of this concern. Over the years, I have seen comparatively few articles that address this silent but formidable threat.

We were good, but I suspect that there are many bad guys out there who are much better at it than we were, and they won't try to get caught in the end as we did. We were also working under a few self-imposed rules that the real bad guys could care less about. Using forced entry, utilizing a crow bar to get through doors or windows, was a no-no for us. Our main tools were a cool head and our social engineering skills. So if we were never detected, despite working under those self-imposed restraints, imagine what a fat ripe target you are for a ruthless, conniving attacker who is playing for high stakes: riches versus prison.

Your organization needs to get its guard up. Toward that end, let me show you a specific example of how I tricked employees into giving me sensitive information. Then we can work on strengthening your defensive posture.

One Step is Better than Two

Sometimes the Social Engineering Gods drop nuggets right into your lap, as Johnny's friend bR00t relays: "I stood on a street corner in Seattle waiting for a bus one day, and I overheard two workers near me discussing their corporate network. One employee described to the other his cool new password, stating it out in the open. He probably assumed this was safe because he felt anonymous. But when I took an incredulous glance back to see what kind of reckless wild man blabs his password on a street corner, there, dangling from a pocket of his cargo pants, was his employee identity badge. There was his name. Right above the logo for Amazon.com, whose headquarters was two buildings away? Amazing. Social engineering can be that easy."

The Mind of a Victim

Any one of us, at any time, could easily become the victim of some form of social engineering. It is not possible to completely eliminate the risk. There are some things that can and should be done to reduce the risk as much as possible, and I'll address some of them later this chapter.

Without some form of training (and practice) in learning how to resist social engineers, you could easily become a victim and not even know it.

Our minds work in very trusting and predictable ways, and that means that exaggerated deviations from the norm might strike us as so improbable, we haven't thought out an appropriate response. This is what social engineers count on. Without awareness of the problem and without an understanding of how our minds can be fooled, there is little defense against social engineering.

"Social engineering would never work against our company!"

That's what a close friend of mine said one afternoon when we were talking about overall security and the threat of social engineering. I had related some of my adventures as a pen-tester, but my friend felt her organization was too sharp for my tricks. "We have good security and our employees wouldn't fall for anyone calling on the phone trying to get information from them," she insisted.

I said, "Give me ninety days so that you won't know when I'm going to call, and I'll test your theory."

She agreed, with one condition. When the attack happened, she wanted me to record it on audio tape and give it to her as a training aid for her to share with her employees. I liked the idea. The contest was on!

I made the call a few weeks later.

"Good afternoon," a friendly voice answered. "Medical Group, this is Mary. Can I help you?"

I immediately put on my doctor hat, "Yes, this is Doctor Wiles," I began. (It's fun saying that even if it is totally fake). "I'm calling to ask a favor. We have a practice similar to yours in Richmond, and we're considering purchasing a new medical billing system. Do you use a fully automated system for your accounting, and if so, do you like it?" My friendly voice didn't raise any suspicion on her part. It was an apparently innocent question.

"Yes we do," she said. "It's called Doctors Database and I believe that they are located in Denver, Colorado."

So far, so good. She seemed willing to talk a little more, so I asked more questions. "Do they offer support when you have problems? We've heard some nightmares from friends who purchased medical billing systems and couldn't get support once they paid for it."

"Yes, we've been very happy with their support," Mary answered.

"How about upgrades and things that need to be fixed? Do they have someone locally that they send to work on the billing system?"

"No, they do everything over a modem that is attached to the system. We've never had a problem with their needing to be here."

I pressed on. "Before we make such a big decision, I'd like to speak with someone from Doctors Database to be sure that this would be the right billing system for us. Could you give me the name and number of the tech support person that you work with when you call them for support? Some of those technical people are very hard to understand. I always feel more comfortable after I've had a chance to speak with the people that our administrator will be working with when problems develop."

Mary apparently had a good working relationship with Doctors Database, because she seemed happy to give me a name. "Yes, we work with Jerry Johnson and he's really easy to talk to. He should be in the office this afternoon if you call before six, east coast time. Their phone number is 800-555-1212 and they have someone available for support by phone twenty-four hours a day."

Little did she know that I now had almost everything that I needed. Just one more question, and I could politely say thanks and goodbye. "I really appreciate your taking the time to help me with this, Mary. After we get the new billing system, would you mind if someone from my office called your database administrator if our administrator has any user questions? It's always easier to ask someone who actually uses the system rather than trying to get the vendor to answer simple questions. I promise that we won't pester you."

She said that she was the administrator of the database and that she would be happy to answer a few questions for us. (It's wonderful living in the friendly sunny south.)

"Thanks so much for helping me with this, Mary," I politely concluded. "I'll be sure to have our administrator call you only if he really gets stuck. Have a great week and thanks again."

What Was I Able to Social Engineer Out of Mary?

This apparently innocent phone call gave me everything that I needed for my final attack. Here's what I got:

- Her name was Mary, and she was the database administrator for the medical office

- They used a medical billing system from a company called Doctors Database, located in Denver, Colorado

- The tech support person that they worked with in Denver was named Jerry Johnson

- Jerry accesses their computer over a modem to work on it

To the casual observer, that's not a lot of dangerous information. Most of it seems to be pretty common knowledge that most people would willingly share. Note that I didn't ask much about her computer, and I certainly didn't ask anything about login IDs, usernames, or passwords.

The Final Sting

Two weeks later, a few minutes before quitting time on a Friday, the phone rang at The Medical Group.

John answered reluctantly on the third ring, knowing that someone calling in that late with a problem could cause him to miss a few precious moments of his three-day weekend. "Good afternoon, The Medical Group, John speaking. May I help you?"

I assumed my best social engineering voice and started my attack. "Hello John, this is Bill Jenkins from Doctors Database in Denver. We're calling all our customers about a serious problem with our medical billing system. It seems that our last update had a virus that we were unaware of until this afternoon. It's causing all of the accounts receivable records to be corrupted. Our entire tech support team is calling our clients as quickly as possible to let them know about the problem. I know that Mary normally works with Jerry Johnson, but he is currently working with another client and has asked me to handle the fix for your system. Can I speak with Mary?"

There was a brief silence. I could feel John quaking at the prospect of squandering the first evening of his three-day weekend. He finally answered. "With the holiday weekend coming up, Mary is off today. I act as her backup on the database work when she off, and I'll try to help if I can."

Things were looking up! I began to spring the trap. "Mary's not there?" I tried to convey a bit of panic in my voice. "John, I'm going to need to log in to your system to fix this, and I don't have Jerry's information in front of me—you know, your modem dial in number, login ID and password. If we need to get those from Mary, we may have a problem. That virus could be loose on your network all weekend." Then I shut up and let the silence do the persuading.

It worked. I could hear him flipping through some papers. "I found it here in her notebook. The phone number is 555-867-5309, the login ID is doctor, and the password is also doctor."

I went into my *good job* routine to make him feel completely at ease. "John, you've been a great help, and I can take it from here. It's been taking about four hours to clean this up and I know that it's Friday afternoon. I don't see any need for you to hang around. I'll install the fix, and things will be back to normal when you get back on Tuesday. Thanks again for your help. Enjoy the weekend!"

When a relieved John hung up, that was probably the last he thought of "Bill Jenkins." You know, until his boss played the tape back for him later.

Why did this scam work?

Without a little bit of awareness training, and a little bit of ongoing suspicion when speaking with strangers on the phone, *anyone* could fall for this kind of an attack.

Many of the hundreds (perhaps thousands) of people who have heard the audio version of this two-part attack have told me that they would have fallen for it as well. That first innocent phone call set the stage for a very believable second phone call where the keys to the kingdom were given away. A lot could have happened to that computer from Friday afternoon until Tuesday morning. Did the real Doctors Database (name changed – this is not their real name) know anything about this incident? Absolutely not! They would have had no idea that a hacker was throwing their name around. Was Jerry Johnson a real person who worked tech support for Doctors Database? Absolutely! Mary worked with him regularly. But Bill Jenkins was a figment of my imagination, carefully placed into a scenario made believable with a generous sprinkling of real facts. Facts that I had socially engineered out of his co-worker.

On top of the social engineering attack vector, the Medical Group's passwords were also extremely insecure. I'm not a big fan of passwords based on words in the dictionary, but that topic falls outside the scope of this book. If you want to pursue it, check out *Perfect Passwords* by Mark Burnett.

Countering Social Engineering Attacks

One of the best defenses against social engineering is awareness. Every employee should be educated on how easily social engineering can be used, the large threat it poses if not detected, and some simple countermeasures. In this section, we'll look at some of the most important things for you to consider as you plan your defense against possible social engineering attacks.

Be Willing To Ask Questions

If there is one thing I was taught at a young age it was to never be afraid to ask questions. If you don't know the answer, ask. This didn't really work during my fourth grade math tests, but everywhere else rendered great results. Asking questions shows intelligence. Not asking because you think you know it all is a sign of fool-headedness. Even if you know the answer, asking questions provides a way to tactfully measure others' knowledge of the topic you may be discussing. People like to assume things as well. I can assume that because you're calling me and asking me a question that you must have some knowledge about the subject, or else why would you be calling me?

Facial and body expressions are also ways that people communicate but this doesn't really help when you're having a conversation on the phone. By asking questions back to any suspicious caller, you will drive away most of them. Ask for a phone number where the caller can be called back. That doesn't guarantee anything, but I've often had potential social engineers hang up after that question. They don't have an untraceable number ready.

Decide ahead of time, and write into policy, what kinds of questions will and will not be answered about the company over the phone. This is an area where employees can get involved. At a monthly meeting, you can stage a "Social Engineering Attack Drill." I've never been fond of role-playing sessions, but this is one area where role-playing is both fun and effective. The incoming caller can be engaged in industrial espionage, competitive spying, intentional destruction, just plain curiosity or any number of things. If the team "defending" the company prepares for the questions that might be asked over the phone, there is a good chance that they will hit on most of the questions that real social engincers ask. When they answer the phone in the role-playing scenarios, they benefit from rehearsing the act of considering carefully before answering questions.

Once our employees were made aware of this threat, their antennas went up as soon as a call came in that was even the slightest bit strange. Your telephonic awareness will improve, too. Of course phone attendants shouldn't be insulting or rude to callers, but it's entirely possible to be firm and alert without sounding impolite. If a caller is legitimate, they may even come to appreciate your willingness to protect company information. Don't you feel safer about making credit card purchases at a store where the cashier politely asks to see your picture ID?

Security Awareness Training

I was surprised to discover that employees really were interested in improving their company's security posture. But it makes sense: if the company succeeds, they succeed. At the very least, their paycheck is assured.

After we ran our security awareness program for awhile, attendees became active participants in the ongoing training. They would send me security-related articles. I was amazed to discover that my training had come full circle. Now, my students had become teachers, and the end result was extremely rewarding for all of us. As the network of informal security proponents grew, security was becoming an interesting challenge instead of a chore.

Posters

As my homegrown awareness seminars took off, so did my awareness poster campaign. I thought it would be a good idea to get the word out through the use of posters, but I wanted to make posters that were effective, eye catching and cheap. My self-imposed criteria also demanded that they be easily reproducible on a standard copy machine. With those thoughts in mind, I sat down with a clip art book and a slightly wild imagination. After about two hours, I had enough clip art drawings, and appropriate clever sayings, to design enough posters for the next two years. I sent out a new poster every three months to a select group of people. It didn't take long for others to call and want to be added to my list for receiving the next poster. Some people started to collect them and line them up along their walls.

Creating posters is easy, but you need to do it right or you won't get results. Remember that the vast majority of employees don't work in IT and thus, don't understand our special jargon, acronyms, and slang. The last thing you want is to make a poster that you think rocks the house, while your target audience thinks it's pointless, mystifying or annoying. You know: "SB1386: It's the Law!" If you're not in IT (and not in California), you would have no idea that the poster is trying to encourage you to bear in mind the state bill that compels businesses to keep their customers' Personally Identifiable Information private.

Here are some of my suggestions for making security posters that people like and remember:

- Use plain language, not acronyms and technical terms that non-IT people don't know.

- One poster, one thought. Don't post a memo of five or ten or twenty important bullet points. That's not memorable, and from more than four inches away, it's not readable, either. There is no worldwide rationing of posters. If you have more to say, you can always make another poster. But try to convey only one idea per poster. Ideally, Keep It Simple Stupid and say it in fewer than fifteen words.

- Involve humor if at all possible. Security is not inherently funny, but if you want a share of your co-workers' minds, humor works far better than attempts to coerce or intimidate.

- Keep an eye on pop culture. Posters based on pirates (*Pirates of the Caribbean*), cartoon characters (*Shrek*, anything Pixar-related) and the like make for popular reminders. All you need is a big imagination, a bit of Photoshop skills, and an eye for security (and how to avoid copyright infringement).

- Emphasize a specific action you want users to take. You could make a poster of a skulking figure, emblazoned with, "Remember: hackers want your password!" But what is an employee supposed to do in response? Better: "Longer is stronger! Choose passwords longer than 14 characters."

- Use posters as reinforcement. Even the World's Best Security Awareness Poster, all by its lonesome self, can't improve your security culture. Posters are best used as reminders that reinforce more in-depth training employees have received.

If you like the notion of making affordable posters but are stuck for catchy ideas, you can find great slogans on line. Check out the clever work by Gary Hinson at www.noticebored.com. Or get more conventional examples at http://www.ussecurityawareness.org/highres/security-awareness.html.

After about six months of sending these posters to whomever wanted one, I received a visit from a stranger I had never seen in our building before. He came to my desk, said hello and introduced himself as a corporate external auditor who was auditing a group in our building. I knew and worked with a number of our own internal auditors, but this was the first real live external auditor that I had ever met. The first few seconds while we were shaking hands, I had that feeling from grade school: "Crap, the Principal has come to visit me; what have I done wrong?" I don't care to experience that intimidated feeling often. But he quickly made me feel at ease by telling me that he wanted to meet whoever came up with these posters. They were so simple and yet so effective that he wanted to take the idea back to his company. I said thanks, and help yourself. (External auditors get whatever that want don't they?) It really drilled home a lesson. You can put up a huge variety of posters, but to an auditor, they all say the same thing: due diligence.

I even started a contest to see who could submit the most interesting poster suggestions for the following year's posters. I had prizes and everything. Just a little imagination and off you go creating your own. Have fun!

Videos

As the demand for my internal security awareness seminars started to increase, I was faced with an ever-growing problem. More and more groups wanted to see the presentation, and I couldn't possibly get to all of them. After all, giving these seminars wasn't even a part of what my immediate group was supposed to do. My next step was to recommend that a video be prepared and used by all of the groups that I couldn't get to. The initial reaction was that it would be too expensive. A studio-quality video can cost over $1,000 per finished minute to create. At those prices, even a 30-minute video would be out of the operating budget for most groups.

I had something much less elaborate in mind. With the help of a friend and a video camera, I created it less than two hours for just about zero cost. Just to see how it would look, we ran the camera during an entire 30-minute session that I presented to a small group. We then created a video of nothing but the slides that were used. The remaining hour was spent editing the two videos together. Our intent was to try this a few times until we got it right. We were trying to come up with something that would be cheap (the most important part at the time) and effective. We had no idea how successful our first attempt would become. Over 100 copies of it were sent all over the company, and most copies were shown a number of times throughout the next year to ensure that everyone had a chance to see it. As far as I know, it is still being shown.

Video Creation Utilities

You may want to check out some software solutions that can assist you in making an awareness video. The Windows-based *Camtasia* product suite from Techsmith (www.techsmith.com) is a great place to start. It can record whatever you are doing on your computer screen and render it as a video – basically, a video screen capture. With voice-over, that's a perfect way to show the do's and don'ts on your network. Mac users may consider Snapz Pro X from Ambrosia Software (www.ambrosiasw.com), also an excellent choice. Both tools allow you to capture on-screen video, presentations and real-time audio. If you're fortunate enough to have a MacBook or MackBook Pro laptop, you can use the built-in video camera to record video footage as well, and iMovie to master your video presentation. Presto! Video without the need for a video camera!

I shared all of this here for a reason. If I can do it, so can you or someone in your company. I learned that homegrown videos are quite popular. In some ways, they gain a certain additional credibility if they are 'real life' and not overly commercial. The equipment to create them is getting more sophisticated and less expensive all the time. If you try this yourself, I think that you will be pleasantly surprised at the outcome.

For examples of an IT department that has made pretty good home-grown security awareness videos for next-to-no money, check out the work by WatchGuard Technology's LiveSecurity team:

WatchGuard Technologies' "Drive-by Download" video
http://video.google.com/videoplay?docid=-3351512772400238297&q=livesecurity
"Contrary Wisdom from Syngress Authors"

This looks expensive but it was shot with two lights, a camera, and a black piece of velvet taped up in a hotel room.

http://video.google.com/videoplay?docid=-2328105253826896657

If you like these, you can see much more by visiting www.video.google.com and searching on "WatchGuard LiveSecurity."

If you are a US citizen, you can also receive free Information Assurance training videos from the Department of Defense. Many are appropriate to show to non-technical employees. For information, visit http://iase.disa.mil/eta/iaetafaq.html.

Certificates

Someone else in the company was pleasantly surprised by my seminars, posters and videos: internal auditors and attorneys. As with the external auditors, the internal guys felt that all this work provided many examples of security-minded due diligence. Our efforts demonstrated that our company was trying its best to prevent computer security violations, both internal and external. In order to help spread the word about the seminars, and to provide further evidence of our commitment to security awareness training, I eventually created a "Certificate of Attendance" that I sent to every attendee.

Even though they are inexpensive to create, the final product can be very professional looking. In fact, as I traveled around the company, I saw a number of them hanging near the desks of former attendees. You can create your own company certificate as easily as I did. All you need is some good certificate stock (blank paper), a word processor and a laser printer. After you experiment with the fonts and word sizes, you can keep a template that only needs to have the names mail merged to create the documents. They will look as professional as any that you will ever see, and you will have one more thing that the internal auditors will love to see hanging on the walls.

Countering the Insider Threat

The insider threat is pervasive. Every statistic that I have ever read on the probability of security violations has pointed towards the "inside" of companies. This attack vector is so complex that I won't be able to do it justice here. For more information, take a look at *Insider Threat: Protecting the Enterprise from Sabotage, Spying, and Theft* by Dr. Eric Cole and Sandra Ring. It's an excellent book about a very important topic.

By searching online, you can also find profiles of the personality types most likely to commit espionage or fraud. The US Army prepared one such document, available at:

http://www.smdc.army.mil/ADR/emotion/emoteT1.htm#Behavior Patterns Associated with Espionage.

How long will you and your company have to continue your awareness campaign? Probably for as long as you continue to work and computers continue to exist. I'm far from a doomsday person, but the more computers pervade every aspect of our lives, the more computer security issues become a major concern.

Security awareness and resistance to social engineering sounds burdensome at first. But it's not. Learning to question strangers and keep your guard up becomes second nature quickly. Think about all the other security behaviors you've learned over your lifetime. You learned not to flash a big roll of cash when you are in crowded places. You learned not to leave your purse unattended on a restaurant table while you visit the restroom. You learned to walk quickly and purposefully when you cross an unsavory part of town. You learned to lock your house when you leave. These are so ingrained into your habits, only the rare person with a mental disorder says, "Because of all the risks, I will never leave my house."

Resistance to social engineering and no-tech hackers can become just as intuitive and ingrained. The key is to stay aware, and remain vigilant in your efforts to inform those around you about the risks and the countermeasures.

Chapter 6

Google Hacking Showcase

A decent no-tech hacker can accumulate a library of significant data just by observing the world around him. But often that data is completely useless on its own. When it comes time to turn data into information, Hollywood tells us that the hacker will have thirty-two plasma screens (divisible by eight, naturally) in his black-walled, red-lighted room that would put NORAD's computer center to shame. In real life, a hacker doesn't even need his own computer to do the necessary research. If he can make it to a public library, Kinko's or Internet cafe, he can use Google to process all that data into something useful. Other times, a hacker will just use Google to troll for targets and sensitive information.

Reprinted from my book *Google Hacking for Penetration Testers*, *Volume Two*, this chapter shows what hackers are capable of when armed only with a search engine and a bit of ingenuity. Be warned though—this is not no-tech hacking, but rather what I'd call low-tech hacking. Still, Google Hacking is an indispensable tool in every no-tech hacker's arsenal, and once you see the examples in this chapter, I think you'll understand why.

Introduction to the Introduction

This chapter is reprinted from my book Google *Hacking for Penetration Testers, Volume 2.* Arguably the most well-known of no-tech hacking techniques among hackers in the know, Google hacking has become a standard weapon in every attacker's arsenal. I'm generally not fond of reprints, but often it's more important to give you the content rather than point you to it–and ask you to pay more hard-earned money for it. So with that in mind, I present this chapter, cobbled together from the now moderately famous *Google Hacking* book. Since this is a reprint, the format and style of this chapter does not match the rest of the book you now hold. I hope you understand. Enjoy. –Johnny

Introduction

A self-respecting Google hacker spends hours trolling the Internet for juicy stuff. Firing off search after search, they thrive on the thrill of finding clean, mean, streamlined queries and get a real rush from sharing those queries and trading screenshots of their findings. I know because I've seen it with my own eyes. As the founder of the Google Hacking Database (GHDB) and the Search engine hacking forums at http://johnny.ihackstuff.com, I am constantly amazed at what the Google hacking community comes up with. It turns out the rumors are true—creative Google searches can reveal medical, financial, proprietary and even classified information. Despite government edicts, regulation and protection acts such as HIPAA, Sarbanes-Oxley, and Graham-Leach-Bliley, and the constant barking of security watchdogs, this problem still persists. Stuff still makes it out onto the Web, and Google hackers snatch it right up.

In my quest to shine a spotlight on the threat, I began speaking on the topic of Google hacking at security conferences such as Black Hat and Defcon. In addition, I was approached to write my first book. After months of writing, I assumed our cause would finally catch the eye of the community at large and that change would be on the horizon. I just knew people would be talking about Google hacking and that awareness about the problem would increase.

Google Hacking, first edition, has made a difference. But nothing made waves like the "Google Hacking Showcase," the fun part of my infamous Google hacking conference talks. The showcase wasn't a big deal to me—it consisted of nothing more than screenshots of wild Google hacks I had witnessed. Borrowing from the pool of interesting Google queries I had created, along with scores of queries from the community; I snagged screenshots and presented them one at a time, making smarmy comments along the way. Every time I presented the showcase, I managed to whip the audience into a frenzy of laughter at the absurd effectiveness of a hacker armed only with a browser and a search engine. It was fun, and it was effective. People talked about those screenshots for months after each talk. They were, after all, the fruits of a Google hacker's labor. Those photos represented the white-hot center of the Google hacking threat.

It made sense then to include the showcase in this edition of *Google Hacking*. In keeping with the original format of the showcase, this chapter will be heavy on photos and light on gab because the photos speak for themselves. Some of the screenshots in this chapter are dated, and some no longer exist on the web, but this is great news. It means that somewhere in the world, someone (perhaps inadvertently) graduated from the level of *googledork* and has taken a step closer to a better security posture.

Regardless, I left in many outdated photos as a stark reminder to those charged with protecting online resources. Those photos serve as proof that this threat is pervasive— it can happen to anyone, and history has shown that it has happened to just about everyone.

So without further ado, enjoy this print version of the Google Hacking Showcase, brought to you by myself and the contributions of the Google Hacking community.

Geek Stuff

This section is about computer stuff. It's about technical stuff, the stuff of geeks. We will take a look at some of the more interesting technical finds uncovered by Google hackers. We'll begin by looking at various utilities that really have no business being online, unless of course your goal is to aid hackers. Then we'll look at open network devices and open applications, neither of which requires any real hacking to gain access to.

Utilities

Any self-respecting hacker has a war chest of tools at his disposal, but the thing that's interesting about the tools in this section is that they are online—they run on a web server and allow an attacker to effectively bounce his reconnaissance efforts off of that hosting web server. To make matters worse, these application-hosting servers were each located with clever Google queries. We'll begin with the handy PHP script shown in Figure 6.1 which allows a web visitor to *ping* any target on the Internet. A *ping* isn't necessarily a bad thing, but why offer the service to anonymous visitors?

Figure 6.1 Php-ping.cgi Provides Free Ping Bounces

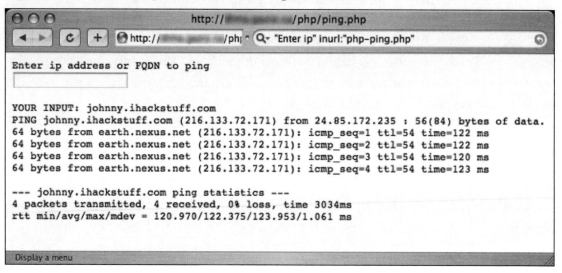

Unlike the *ping* tool, the *finger* tool has been out of commission for quite a long time. This annoying service allowed attackers to query users on a UNIX machine, allowing enumeration of all sorts of information such as user connect times, home directory, full name and more. Enter the *finger* CGI script, an awkward attempt to "webify" this irritating service. As shown in Figure 6.2, a well-placed Google query locates installations of this script, providing web visitors with a *finger* client that allows them to query the service on remote machines.

Figure 6.2 Finger CGI Script Allows Remote Fingering

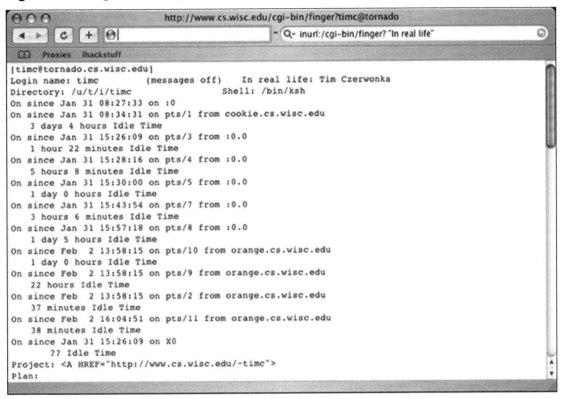

Pings and *finger* lookups are relatively benign; most system administrators won't even notice them traversing their networks. *Port scans*, on the other hand, are hardly ever considered benign, and a paranoid administrator (or piece of defense software) will take note of the source of a port scan. Although most modern port scanners provide options which allow for covert operation, a little Google hacking can go a long way. Figure 6.3 reveals a Google search submitted by Jimmy Neutron which locates sites that will allow a web visitor to portscan a target.

Figure 6.3 PHPPort Scanner- A Nifty Web-Based Portscanner

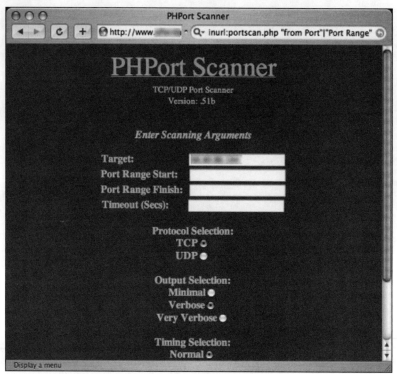

Remember, scans performed in this way will originate from the web server, not from the attacker. Even the most paranoid system administrator will struggle to trace a scan launched in this way. Of course, most attackers won't stop at a portscan. They will most likely opt to continue probing the target with any number of network utilities which could reveal their true location. However, if an attacker locates a web page like the one shown in Figure 6.4 (submitted by Jimmy Neutron), he can channel various network probes through the *WebUtil* Perl script hosted on that remote server. Once again, the probes will appear to come from the web server, not from the attacker.

Figure 6.4 WebUtil Lets An Attacker Do Just About Anything

The web page listed in Figure 6.5 (submitted by Golfo) lists the name, address and device information for a school's "student enrollment" systems. Clicking through the interface reveals more information about the architecture of the network, and the devices connected to it. Consolidated into one easy-to-read interface and located with a Google search, this page makes short work of an attacker's reconnaissance run.

Figure 6.5 WhatsUp Status Screen Provides Guests with a Wealth of Information

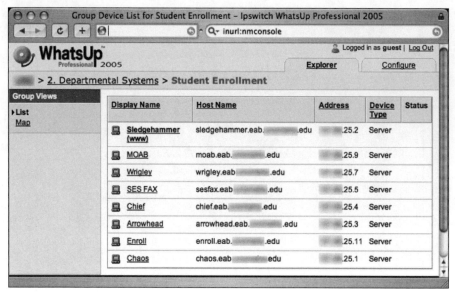

Open Network Devices

Why hack into a network server or device when you can just point and click your way into an *open* network device? Management devices, like the one submitted by Jimmy Neutron in Figure 6.6, often list all sorts of information about a variety of devices.

Figure 6.6 Open APC Management Device

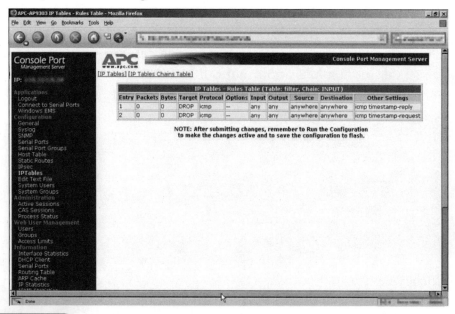

When m00d submitted the query shown in Figure 6.7, I honestly didn't think much of it. The SpeedStream router is a decidedly lightweight device installed by home users, but I was startled to find them sitting wide-open on the Internet. I personally like the button in the point-to-point summary listing. Who do you want to disconnect today?

Figure 6.7 Open SpeedStream DSL Router Allows Remote Disconnects

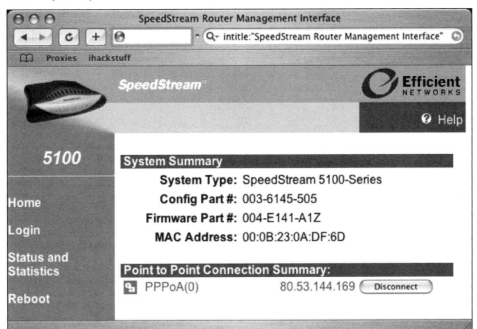

Belkin is a household name in home network gear. With their easy-to-use web-based administrative interfaces, it makes sense that eventually pages like the one in Figure 6.8 would get crawled by Google. Even without login credentials, this page reveals a ton of information that could be interesting to a potential attacker. I got a real laugh out of the *Features* section of the page. The firewall is enabled, but the wireless interface is wide open and unencrypted. As a hacker with a social conscience, my first instinct is to enable encryption on this access point—in an attempt to protect this poor home user from themselves.

Figure 6.8 Belkin Router Needs Hacker Help

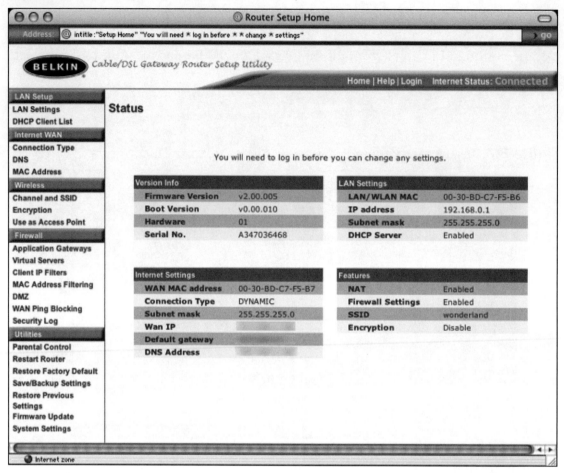

Milkman brings us the query shown in Figure 6.9, which digs up the configuration interface for Smoothwall personal firewalls. There's something just wrong about Google hacking someone's firewall.

Figure 6.9 Smoothwall Firewall Needs Updating

As Jimmy Neutron reveals in the next two figures, even big-name gear like Cisco shows up in the recesses of Google's cache every now and again. Although it's not much to look at, the switch interface shown in Figure 6.10 leaves little to the imagination—all the configuration and diagnostic tools are listed right on the main page.

Figure 6.10 Open Cisco Switch

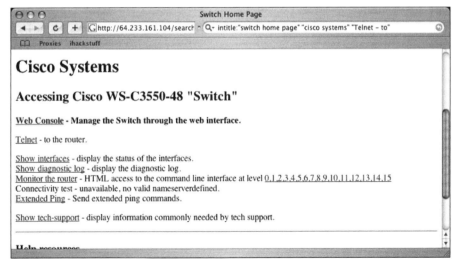

This second Cisco screenshot should look familiar to Cisco geeks. I don't know why, but the Cisco nomenclature reminds me of a bad Hollywood flick. I can almost hear the grating voice of an over-synthesized computer beckoning, "Welcome to Level 15."

Figure 6.11 Welcome to Cisco Level 15

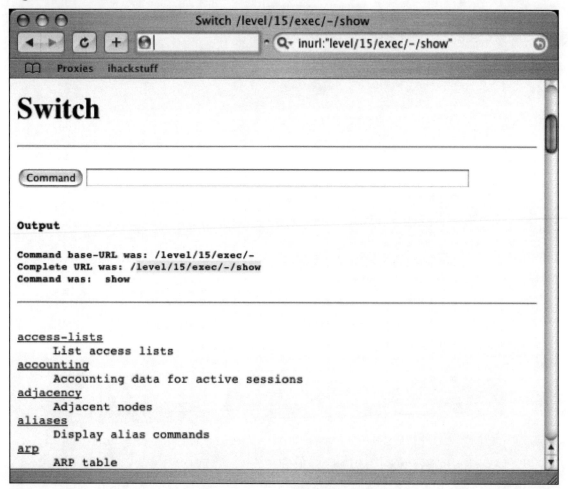

The search shown in Figure 6.12 (submitted by Murfie) locates interfaces for an Axis network print server. Most printer interfaces are really boring, but this one in particular piqued my interest. First, there's the button named *configuration wizard*, which I'm pretty sure launches a configuration wizard. Then there's the handy link labeled *Print Jobs*, which lists the print jobs. In case you haven't already guessed, Google hacking sometimes leaves little to the imagination.

Figure 6.12 Axis Print Server with Obscure Buttonage

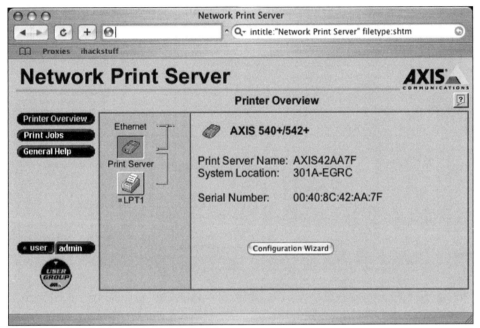

Printers aren't entirely boring things. Consider the *Web Image Monitor* shown in Figure 6.13. I particularly like the document on *Recent Religion Work*. That's quite an honorable pursuit, except when combined with the document about *Aphrodisiacs*. I really hope the two documents are unrelated. Then again, nothing surprises me these days.

Figure 6.13 Ricoh Print Server Mixes Religion and Aphrodisiacs

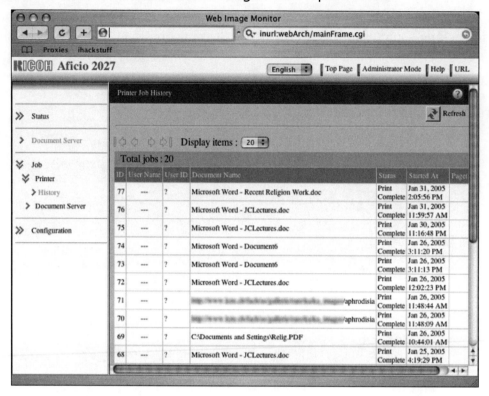

CP has a way of finding Google hacks that make me laugh, and Figure 6.14 is no exception. Yes, this is the web-based interface to a municipal water fountain.

Figure 6.14 Hacking Water Fountains For Fun and Profit

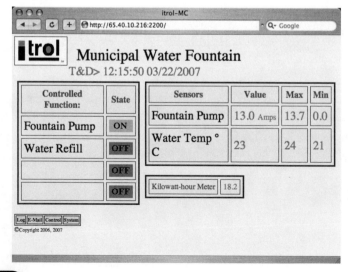

After watching the water temperature fluctuate for a few intensely boring seconds, it's only logical to click on the *Control* link to see if it's possible to actually control the municipal water fountain. As Figure 6.15 reveals, yes it is possible to remotely control the municipal water fountain.

Figure 6.15 More Water Fountain Fun

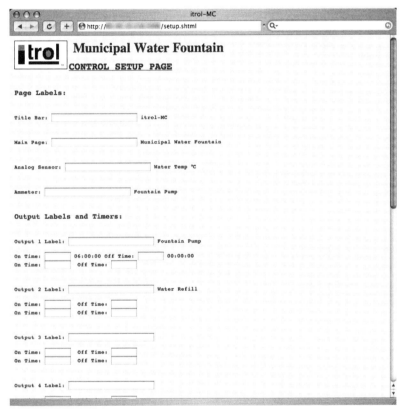

One bit of advice though—if you happen to bump into one of these, be nice. Don't go rerouting the power into the water storage system. I think that would definitely constitute an act of terrorism.

Moving along to a more traditional network fixture, consider the screenshot captured in Figure 6.16.

Figure 6.16 An IDS Manager on Acid

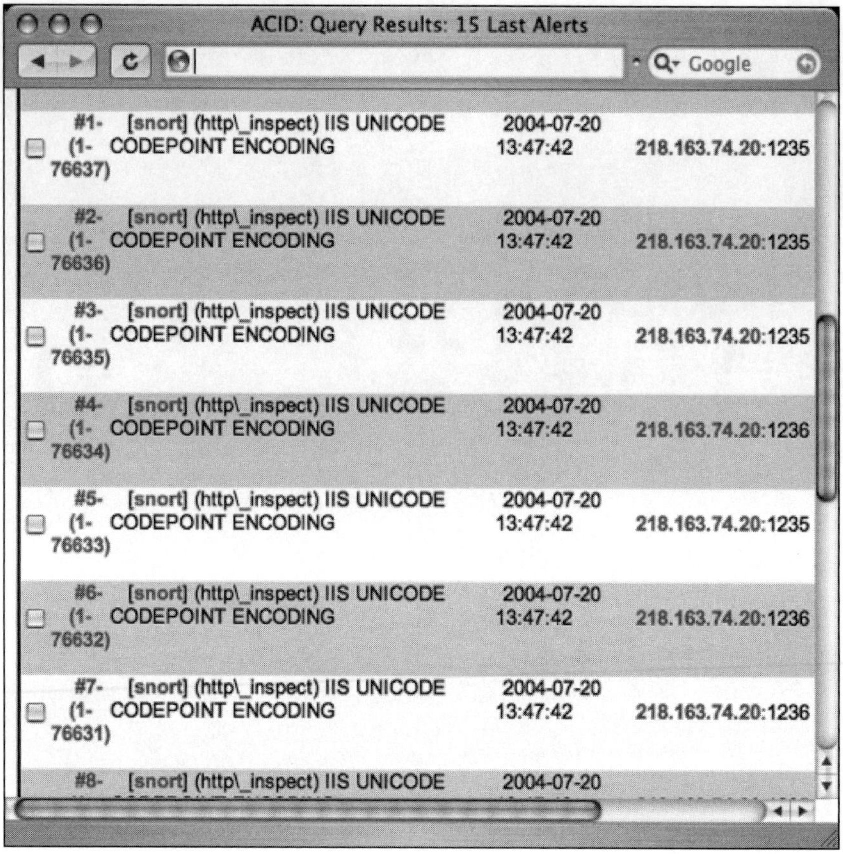

Now, I've been in the security business for a lot of years, and I'm not exactly brilliant in any one particular area of the industry. But I do know a little bit about a lot of different things, and one thing I know for sure is that security products are designed to protect stuff. It's the way of things. But when I see something like the log shown in Figure 6.16, I get all confused. See, this is a web-based interfaced for the Snort intrusion detection system. The last time I checked, this data was supposed to be kept away from the eyes of an attacker, but I guess I missed an email or something. But I suppose there's logic to this somewhere. Maybe if the attacker sees his screw-ups on a public webpage, he'll be too ashamed to ever hack again, and he'll go on to lead a normal productive life. Then again, maybe he and his hacker buddies will just get a good laugh out of his good fortune. It's hard to tell.

Open Applications

Many mainstream web applications are relatively idiot-proof, designed for the point-and-click masses that know little about security. Even still, the Google hacking community has discovered hundreds of online apps that are wide open, just waiting for a point-and-click script kiddy to come along and own them. The first in this section was submitted by Shadowsliv and is shown in Figure 6.17.

Figure 6.17 Tricky Pivot Hack Requires Five Correct Field Fills

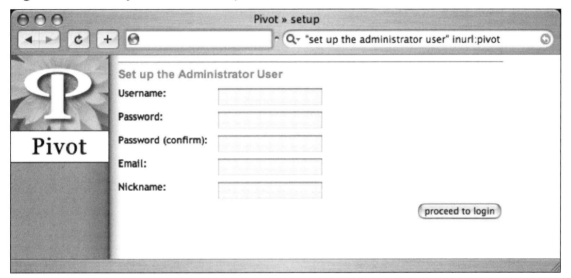

The bad news is that if a hacker can figure out what to type in those confusing fields, he'll have his very own Pivot web log. The good news is that most skilled attackers will leave this site alone, figuring that any software left this unprotected *must* be a honeypot. It's really sad that hacking (not *real* hacking mind you) can be reduced to a point-and-click affair, but as Arrested's search reveals in Figure 6.18, owning an entire website can be a relatively simple affair.

Figure 6.18 PHP-Nuke Ownage in Four Correct Field Fills

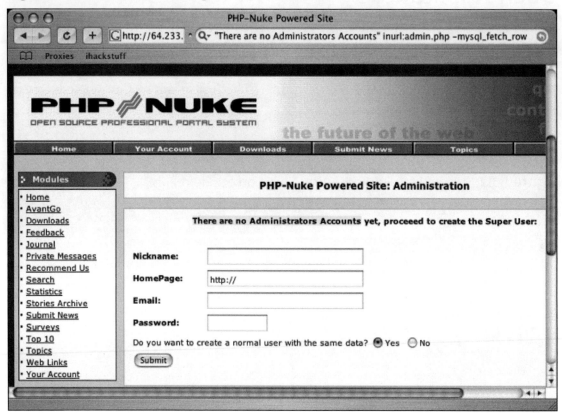

Sporting one less field than the open Pivot install, this configuration page will create a PHP-Nuke Administrator account, and allow any visitor to start uploading content to the page as if it were their own. Of course, this takes a bit of malicious intent on behalf of the web visitor. There's no mistaking the fact that he or she is creating an Administrator account on a site that does not belong to them. However, the text of the page in Figure 6.19 is a bit more ambiguous.

Figure 6.19 Hack This PHP-Nuke Install "For Security Reasons"

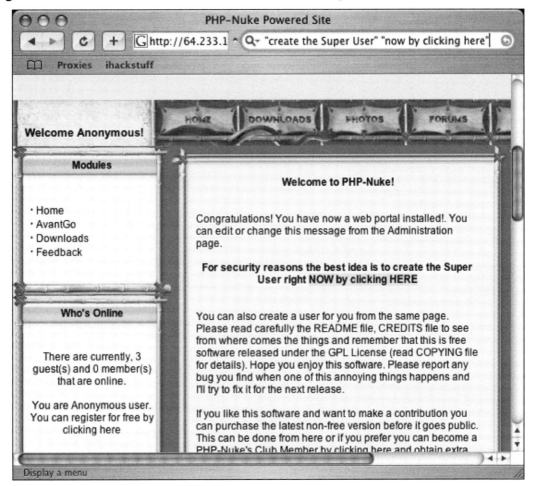

The bold text in the middle of the page really cracks me up. I can just imagine somebody's poor Grandma running into this page and reading it aloud. "For security reasons, the best idea is to create the Super User right NOW by clicking HERE." I mean who in their right mind would avoid doing something that was for *security reasons*? For all Grandma knows, she may be saving the world from evil hackers ... by hacking into some poor fool's PHP-Nuke install.

And as if owning a website isn't cool enough, Figure 6.20 (submitted by Quadster) reveals a phpMyAdmin installation logged in as root, providing unfettered access to a MySQL database.

Figure 6.20 Open phpMyAdmin - MySQL Ownage for Dummies

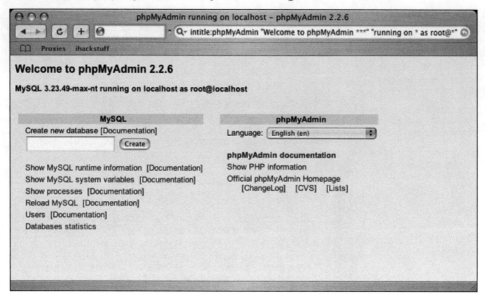

With a website install and an SQL database under his belt, it's a natural progression for a Google hacker to want the ultimate control of a system. VNC installations provide remote control of a system's keyboard and mouse. Figure 6.21, submitted by Lester, shows a query that locates RealVNC's Java-based client.

Figure 6.21 Hack A VNC, Grab A Remote Keyboard

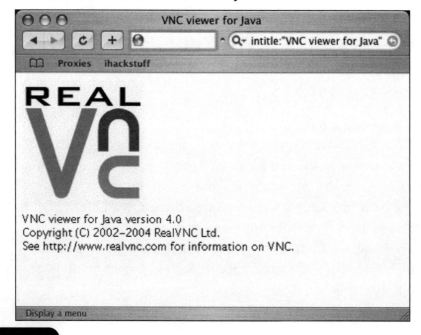

Locating a client is only part of the equation, however. An attacker will still need to know the address, port and (optional) password for a VNC server. As Figure 6.22 reveals, the Java client itself often provides two-thirds of that equation in a handy popup window.

Figure 6.22 VNC Options Handed Up with a Side of Fries

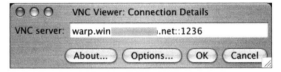

If the hacker really lucks out and stumbles on a server that's not password protected, he's faced with the daunting task of figuring out which of the four buttons to click in the above connection window. Here's a hint for the script kiddie looking to make his way in the world: it's not the *Cancel* button.

Of course running without a password is just plain silly. But passwords can be so difficult to remember and software vendors obviously realize this as evidenced by the password prompt shown in Figure 6.23.

Figure 6.23 Handy Password Reminder, In Case The Hacker Forgot

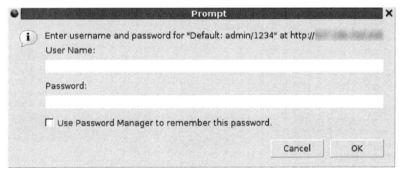

Posting the default username/password combination on a login popup is just craziness. Unfortunately it's not an isolated event. Check out Figure 6.24, submitted by Jimmy Neutron. Can you guess the default password?

Figure 6.24 You Suck If You Can't Guess This Default Password

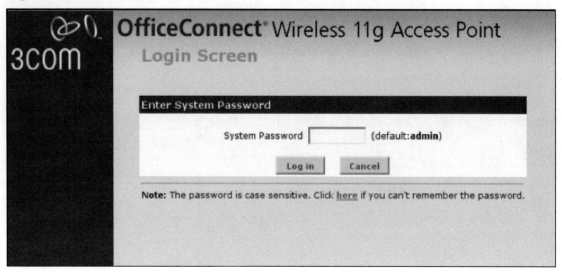

Graduating to the next level of hacker leetness requires a bit of work. Check out the user screen shown in Figure 6.25, which was submitted by Dan Kaminsky.

Figure 6.25 Welcome To Guest Access

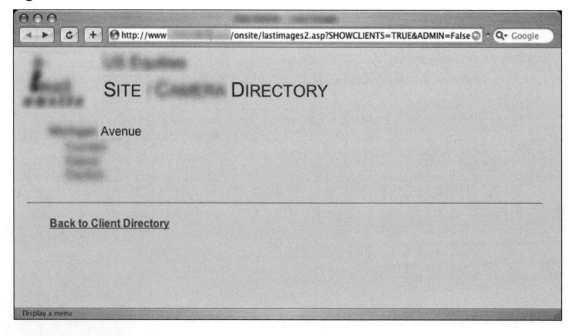

If you look carefully, you'll notice that the URL contains a special field called *ADMIN*, which is set to *False*. Think like a hacker for a moment and imagine how you might gain administrative access to the page. The spoiler is listed in Figure 6.26.

Figure 6.26 Admin Access through URL Tinkering

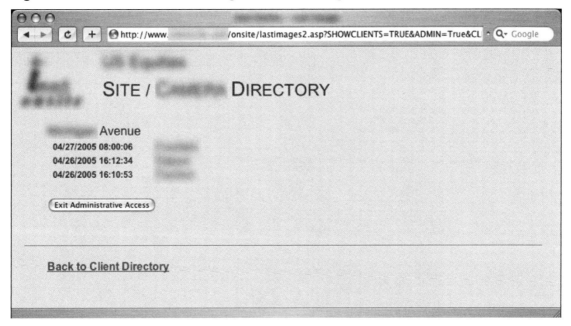

Check out the shiny new *Exit Administrative Access* button. By Changing the *ADMIN* field to *True*, the application drops us into Administrative access mode. Hacking really is hard, I promise.

Cameras

I've got to be honest and admit that like printer queries, I'm really sick of webcam queries. For a while there, every other addition to the GHDB was a webcam query. Still, some webcam finds are pretty interesting and worth mentioning in the showcase. I'll start with a cell phone camera dump, submitted by Vipsta as shown in Figure 6.27.

Figure 6.27 Google Crawled Vehicular Carnage

Not only is this an interesting photo of some pretty serious-looking vehicular carnage, but the idea that Google trolls camera phone picture sites is interesting. Who knows what kind of blackmail fodder lurks in the world's camera phones. Not that anyone would ever use that kind of information for sensationalistic or economically lucrative purposes. Ahem.

Moving on, check out the office-mounted open web camera submitted by Klouw as shown in Figure 6.28.

Figure 6.28 Remote Shoulder Surfing 101

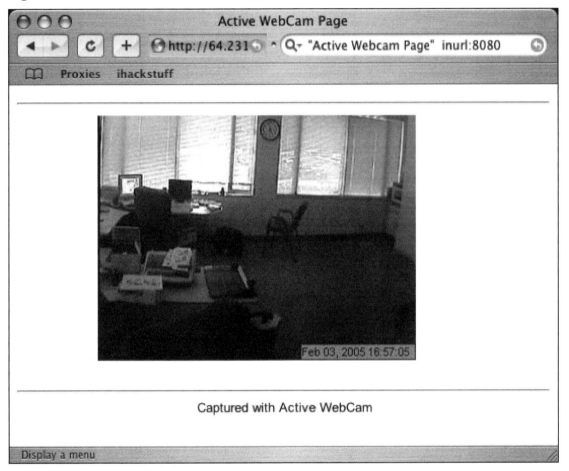

This is really an interesting web cam. Not only does it reveal all the activity in the office, but it seems especially designed to allow remote shoulder surfing. Hackers used to have to get out of the house to participate in this classic sport. These days all they have to do is fire off a few Google searches.

Figure 6.29, submitted by Jimmy Neutron, shows the I.T. infrastructure of a tactical US nuclear submarine.

Figure 6.29 Not Really A Tactical US Nuclear Submarine

OK, so not really. It's probably just a nuclear reactor or power grid control center or even a drug lord's warehouse in Columbia (Maryland). Or maybe I've been reading too many *Stealing The Network* books. Either way, it's a cool find none the less.

Figure 6.30, however (submitted by JBrashars) is unmistakable. It's definitely a parking lot camera. I'm not sure why, exactly, a camera is pointed at a handicapped parking space, but my guess is that there have been reports of handicapped parking spot abuse. Imagine the joy of being the guard that gets to witness the CIO parking in the spot, leaping out of his convertible and running into the building. Those are the stories of security guard legends.

Figure 6.30 Handicapped Parking Spot Gestapo Cam

WarriorClown sent me the search used for the capture shown in Figure 6.31. It shows what appears to be a loading dock, and a field of white explosive containers.

Figure 6.31 Remote Exploding Container Fun

Although it looks pretty boring at first, this webcam is really a lot of fun. Check out the interesting button in the upper right of the capture. I'm pretty sure that clicking on that button fires a laser beam at the explosive white containers, which creates maximum carnage, but can only be done once – unless you set them to respawn, which will bring them back automatically. Oh, wait. That only works in Halo 3's Forge mode. OK, all these webcams are starting to make me loopy. In an attempt to get my imagination in check, I present pretty straightforward security camera view shown in Figure 6.32.

Figure 6.32 Open Web "Security" Cameras

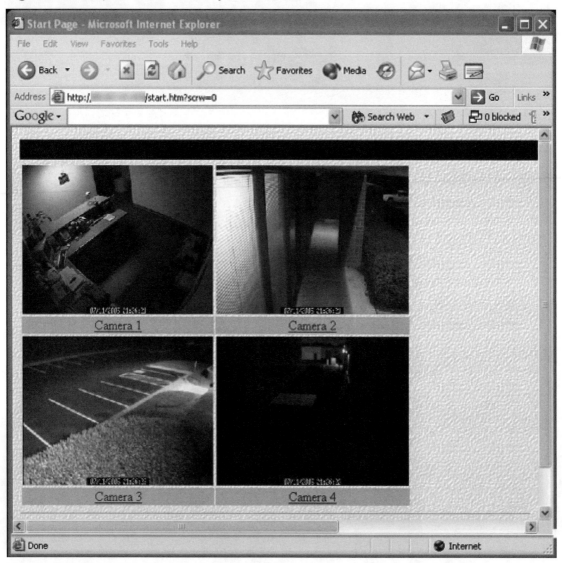

I can't be the only one that thinks it's insane to put open security camera feeds on the Internet. Of course it happens in Hollywood movies all the time. It seems the first job for the hired hacker is to tap into the video surveillance feeds. But the movies make it look all complicated and technical. I've never once seen a Hollywood hacker use Google to hack the security system. Then again, that wouldn't look nearly as cool as using fiber optic cameras, wire cutters and alligator clips.

Moving on, the search shown in Figure 6.33 (submitted by JBrashars) returns quite a few hits for open Everfocus EDSR applets.

Figure 6.33 EDSR Sounds Tame Enough

The Everfocus EDSR is a multi-channel digital video recording system with a web-based interface. It's a decent surveillance product, and as such it is password protected by default, as shown in Figure 6.34.

Figure 6.34 Password Protection: The Gold Standard of Security

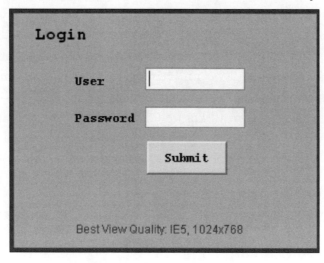

Unfortunately, as revealed by an anonymous contributor, the factory-default administrative username and password provides access to many of these systems, as shown in Figure 6.35.

Figure 6.35 Welcome to Surveillance Central

Once inside, the EDSR applet provides access to multiple live video feeds and a historic record of any previously recorded activity. Again, just like the magic of Hollywood without all the hacker smarts.

The EDSR isn't the only multi-channel video system that is targeted by Google hackers. As Murfie reveals, a search for I-catcher CCTV returns many systems like the one shown in Figure 6.36.

Figure 6.36 Housekeeper Needed. Apply Within

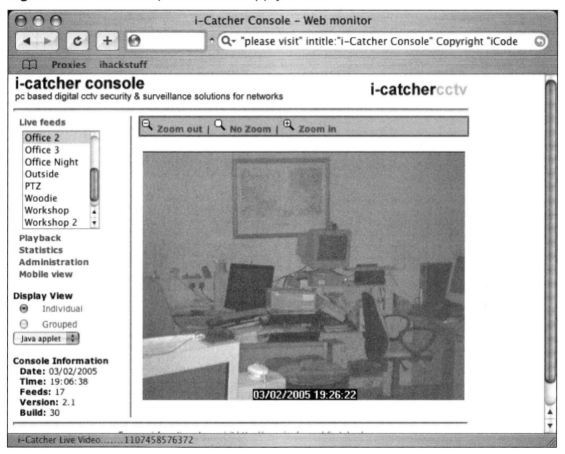

Although the interface may look simple, it provides access to multiple live camera views, including one called "Woodie" which I was personally afraid to click on.

These cameras are all interesting, but I've saved my favorite for last. Check out Figure 6.37.

Figure 6.37 Shoulder Surfing Meets Webcam Meets Password Stickers

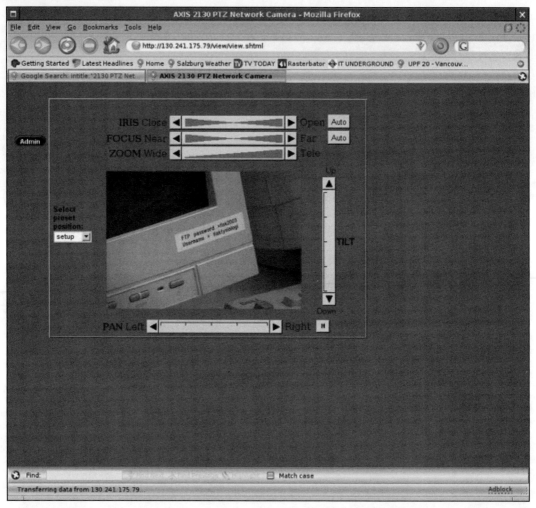

This camera provides open access to web visitors. Located in a computer lab, the camera's remote control capability allows anonymous visitors to peer around, panning and zooming to their hearts content. Not only does this allow for some great shoulder surfing, but the sticker in the above screen capture had me practically falling out of my chair. It lists a username and password for the lab's online FTP server. Stickers listing usernames and passwords are bad enough, but I wonder whose bright idea it was to point an open webcam at them?

Telco Gear

I've never been much of a phreaker (phone hacker), but thanks to the depth of Google's searching capabilities, I wouldn't need to have much experience to get into this shady line of work. As JBrashar's search reveals in Figure 6.38, the surge of Voice over IP (VOIP) service has resulted in a host of new web-based phone interfaces.

Figure 6.38 Google Hacking Residential Phone Systems

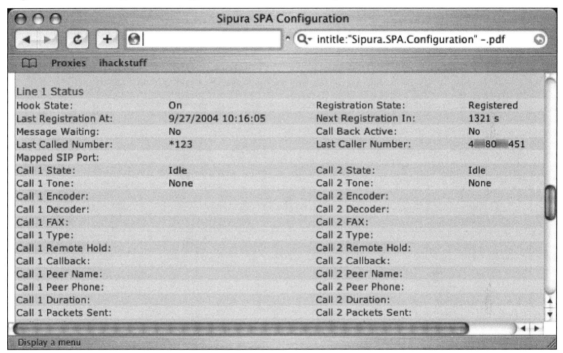

It's interesting to me that by just using Google, an attacker could get phone history information such as last called number and last caller number. Normally, the Sipura SPA software does a better job of protecting this information, but this particular installation is improperly configured. Other, more technical information can also be uncovered by clicking through the links on the web interface, as shown in Figure 6.39.

Figure 6.39 Redux

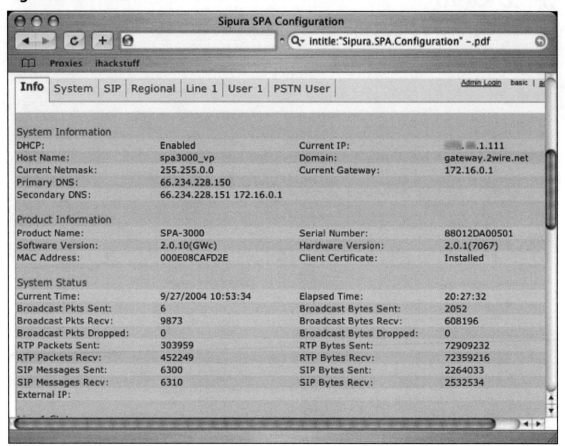

There are so many VOIP devices that it's impossible to cover them all, but the new kid on the VOIP server block is definitely Asterisk. After checking out the documentation for the Asterisk management portal, Jimmy Neutron uncovered the interesting search shown in Figure 6.40.

Figure 6.40 Asterisk, King of the VOIP

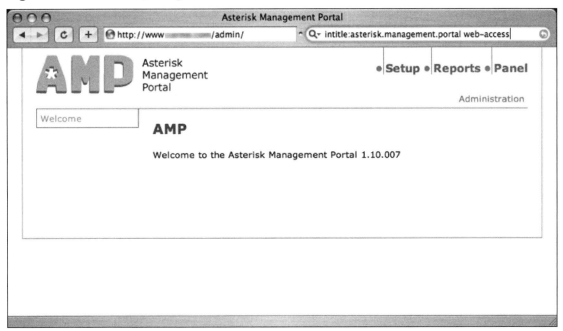

From this open, an attacker can make changes to the Asterisk server, including forwarding incoming calls, as shown in Figure 6.41.

Figure 6.41 Google Hacking Asterisk Management Portals

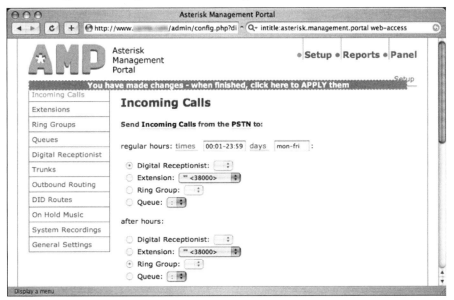

Unfortunately, a hacker's fun wouldn't necessarily stop there. It's simple to re-route extensions, monitor or re-route voicemail, enable or disable digital receptionists and even upload disturbing on-hold music. But Jimmy's Asterisk VOIP digging didn't stop there; he later submitted the search shown in Figure 6.42.

Figure 6.42 Redux. HackenBush. Heh

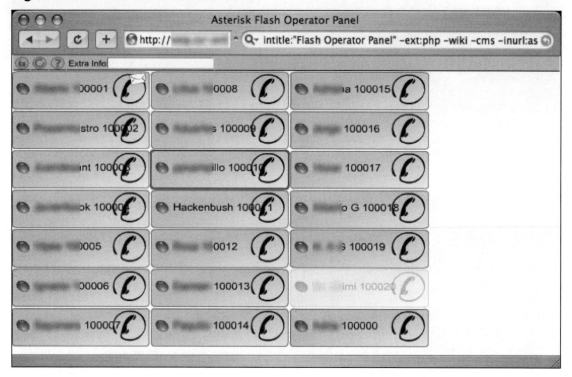

This flash-based operator panel provides access to similar capabilities, and once again, the interface was found open to any Internet visitor.

Moving along, Yeseins serves up the interesting search shown in Figure 6.43, which locates videoconferencing management systems.

Figure 6.43 Hacking Videoconference Systems?

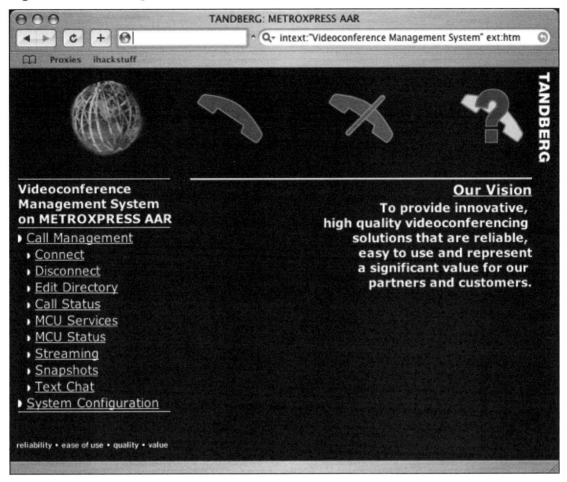

This management system allows a web visitor to connect, disconnect and monitor conference calls, take snapshots of conference participants, and even change line settings as shown in Figure 6.44.

Figure 6.44 Redirecting Videoconference Lines

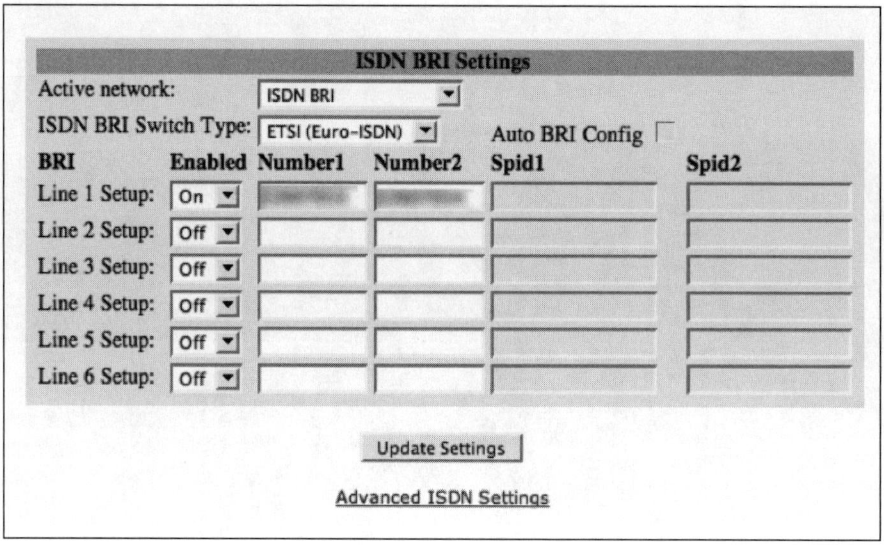

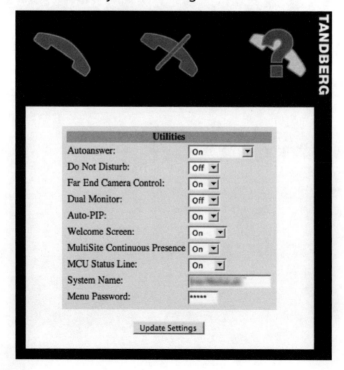

A malicious hacker could even change the system name and password, locking legitimate administrators out of their own system, as shown in Figure 6.45.

Figure 6.45 Videoconference System Ownage

Despite all the new-fangled web interfaces we've looked at, Google hacking bridges the gap to older systems as well, as shown in Figure 6.46.

Figure 6.46 Google Phreaking Old School Style

This front-end was designed to put a new face on an older PBX product, but client security seems to have been an afterthought. Notice that the interface asks the user to "Logout" of the interface, indicating that the user is already logged in. Also, notice that cryptic button labeled *Start Managing the Device*. After firing off a Google search, all a malicious hacker has to do is figure out which button to press. What an unbelievably daunting task.

Power

I get a lot of raised eyebrows when I talk about using Google to hack power systems. Most people think I'm talking about UPS systems like the one submitted by Yeseins in Figure 6.47.

Figure 6.47 Whazzups?

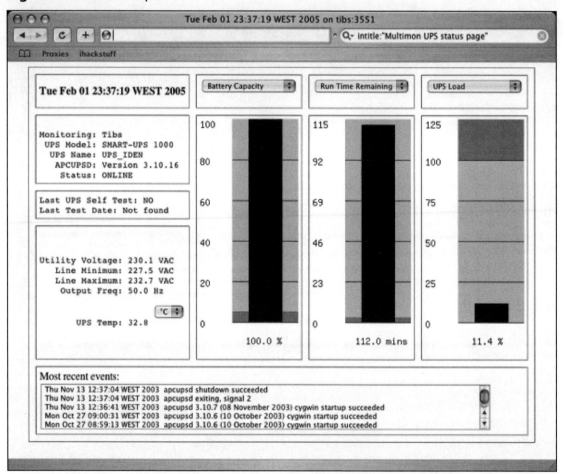

This is a clever Google query, but it's only an uninterruptible power system (UPS) monitoring page. This can be amusing, but as Jimmy Neutron shows in Figure 6.48, there are more interesting power hacking opportunities available.

Figure 6.48 Bedroom Hacking For Dummies

AMX NetLinx systems are designed to allow control of power systems. The figure above seems to suggest that a web visitor could control power in a theater, a family room and the master bedroom of a residence. The problem is that the Google search turns up a scarce number of results, most of which are password protected. As an alternative, Jimmy offers the search shown in Figure 6.49.

Figure 6.49 Passwords Are Nifty, Especially Default Ones

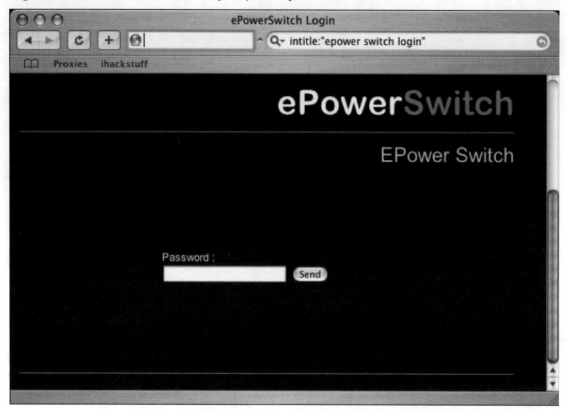

Although this query results in a long list of password-protected sites, many sites still use the default password, providing access to the control panel shown in Figure 6.50.

Figure 6.50 Google Hacking Light Sockets? Uh oh

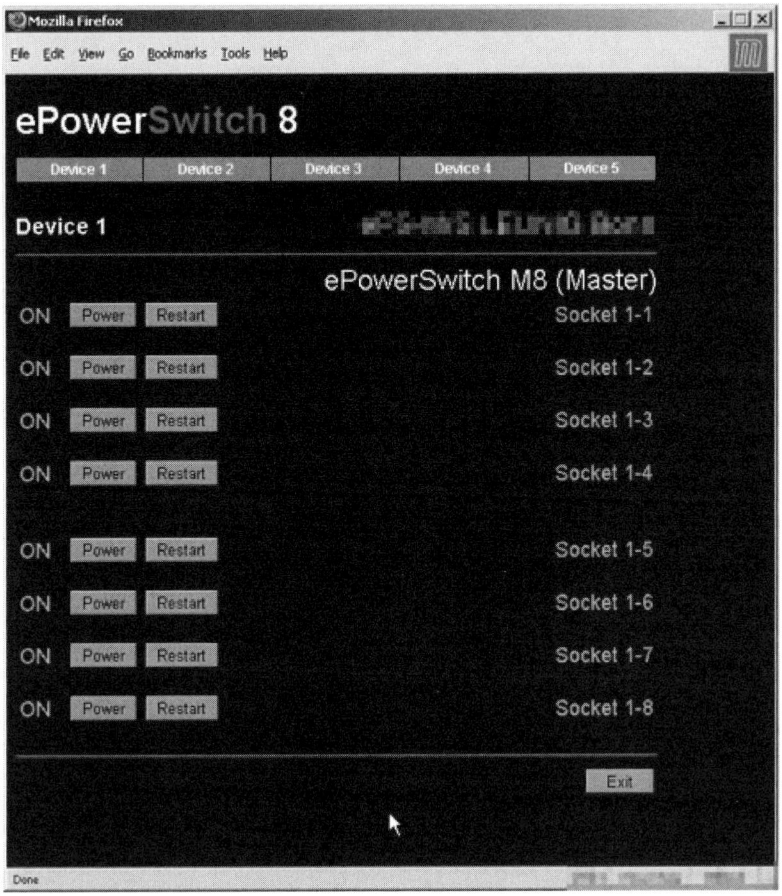

This control panel lists power sockets alongside interesting buttons named *Power* and *Restart*, which even the dimmest of hackers will undoubtedly be able to figure out. The problem with this interface is that it's just not much fun. A hacker will definitely get bored flipping unnamed power switches – unless of course he also finds an open webcam so he can watch the fun. The search shown in Figure 6.51 seems to address this, naming each of the devices for easy reference.

Figure 6.51 Step Away From The Christmas Lights

Of course even the most vicious hackers would probably consider it rude to nail someone's Christmas lights, but no hacker in their right mind could resist the open HomeSeer control panel shown in Figure 6.52.

Figure 6.52 Bong Hacking. BONG Hacking

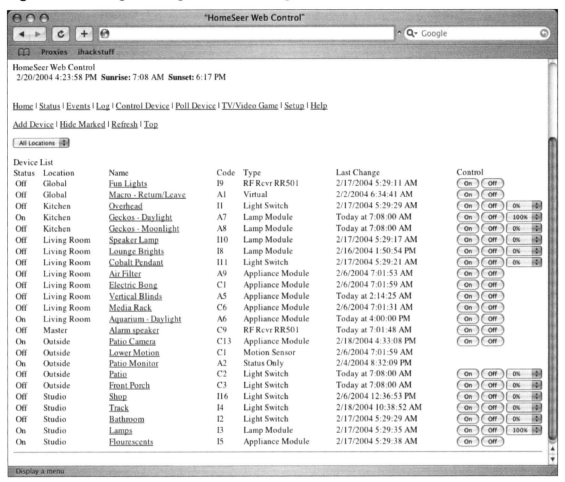

The HomeSeer control panel puts the fun back into power hacking, listing descriptions for each control, as well as an *On*, *Off* and slider switch for applicable elements. Some of the elements in this list are quite interesting, including *Lower Motion* and *Bathroom*. The best though is definitely *Electric Bong*. If you're a member of the Secret Service looking to bust the owner of this system, I would suggest a preemptive Google strike before barging into the home. Start by dimming the lights, and then nail the motion sensors. Last but not least, turn on the electric bong in case your other charges don't stick.

Sensitive Info

Sensitive info is such a generic term, but that's what this section includes: a hodgepodge of sensitive info discovered while surfing Google. We'll begin with the VCalendar search submitted by Jorokin as shown in Figure 6.53.

Figure 6.53 Let Me Check Their Calendar

There's at least a decent possibility that these calendar files were made public on purpose, but the Netscape history file submitted by Digital_Revolution in Figure 6.54 shouldn't be public.

Figure 6.54 Hot Chicks at IBM? Nah

For starters, the file contains the user's POP email username and encoded password. Then there's the issue of his URL history, which contains not only the very respectable *IBM.com*, but also the not-so-respectable *hotchicks.com,* which I'm pretty sure is *NSFW.*

Next up is an MSN contact list submitted by Harry-AAC, which is shown in Figure 6.55.

Figure 6.55 Want To Steal My Friends?

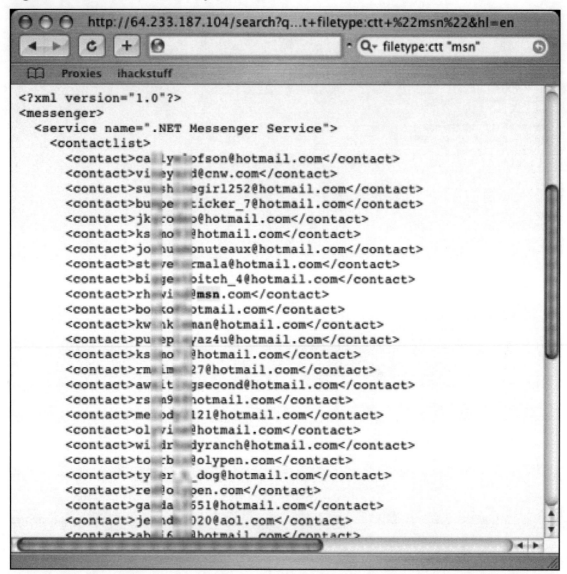

This file lists the contact names and email addresses found in someone's contact list. At best, this file is spam fodder. There's really no shortage of email address lists, phone number lists and more on the Web, but what's surprising is how many documents containing this type of information were created with the express intention of sharing that information. Consider the screen shown in Figure 6.56, which was submitted by CP.

Figure 6.56 Call and Email the Entire Staff and Wish Them Happy Birthday

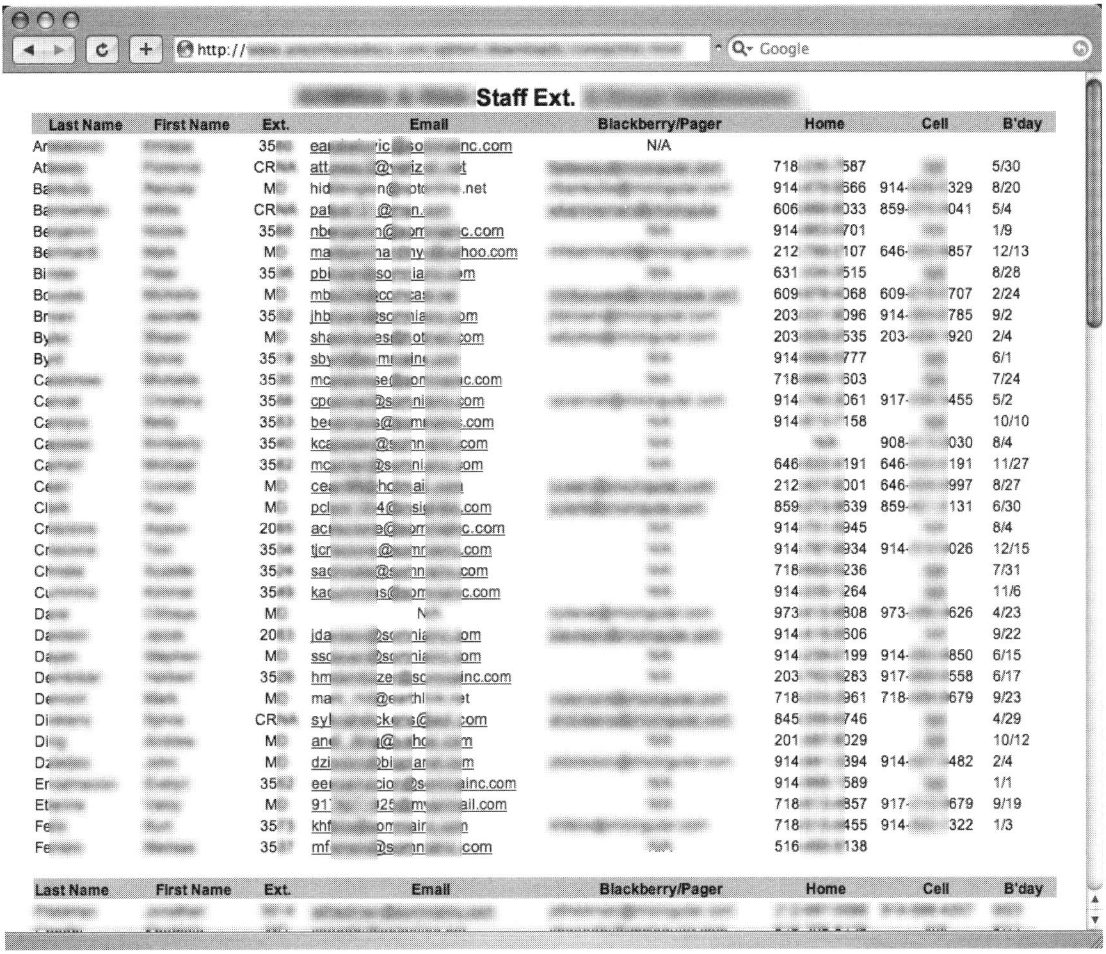

This document is a staff directory, which was created for internal use only. The only problem is that it was found on a public web site. While this doesn't seem to constitute seriously private information, the search shown in Figure 6.57 (submitted by Maerim) reveals slightly more sensitive information: passwords.

Figure 6.57 I Think This RCON Password is Written In Greek

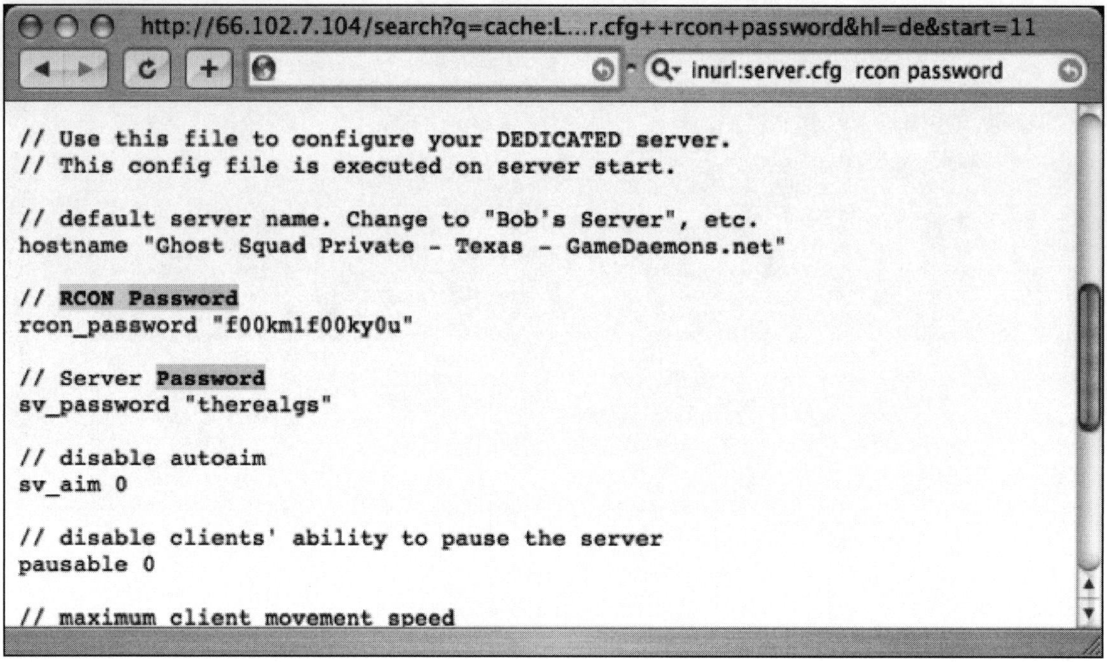
http://66.102.7.104/search?q=cache:L...r.cfg++rcon+password&hl=de&start=11
inurl:server.cfg rcon password
// Use this file to configure your DEDICATED server.
// This config file is executed on server start.
// default server name. Change to "Bob's Server", etc.
hostname "Ghost Squad Private - Texas - GameDaemons.net"
// RCON Password
rcon_password "f00kmlf00ky0u"
// Server Password
sv_password "therealgs"
// disable autoaim
sv_aim 0
// disable clients' ability to pause the server
pausable 0
// maximum client movement speed

This file lists the cleartext passwords for the Ghost Squad's *private* Counterstrike remote administration console. Ask any GS gamer how embarrassing this could be. But hacking a game server is fairly tame. Consider, however, Figure 6.58 which was submitted by Barabas.

Figure 6.58 Encoded VPN Passwords

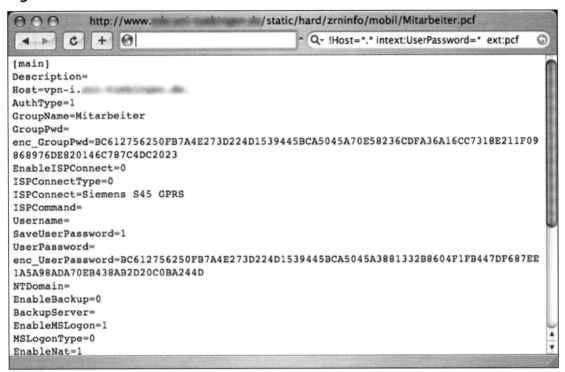

This file lists information and encoded passwords for a Cisco Virtual LAN (VLAN). About the only thing worse than revealing your VLAN's encoded passwords is revealing your VLAN's *cleartext* passwords. Ask and you shall receive. Check out Figure 6.59, again from Barabas.

Figure 6.59 Plaintext VPN Passwords

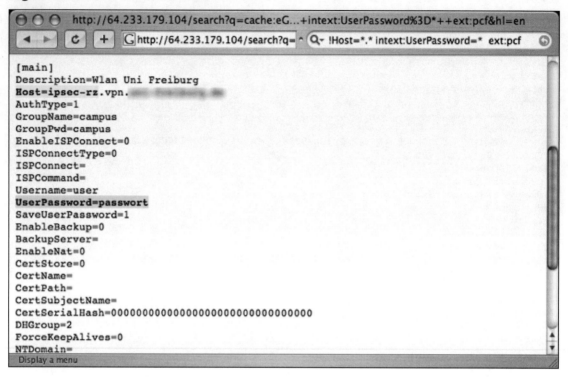

Yup, that's a cleartext password nestled inside a University's configuration file. But interesting passwords can be found in all sorts of places, such as inside Windows unattended installation files, as shown in Figure 6.60, which was submitted by MBaldwin.

Figure 6.60 Owning a Windows Install before It's Installed. Leet

This file also reveals the product key of the installed software, which could be re-used to install the software illegally. Last but not least, check out Figure 6.61, submitted by CP.

Figure 6.61 Hey, Can I Get All Your Web Passwords?

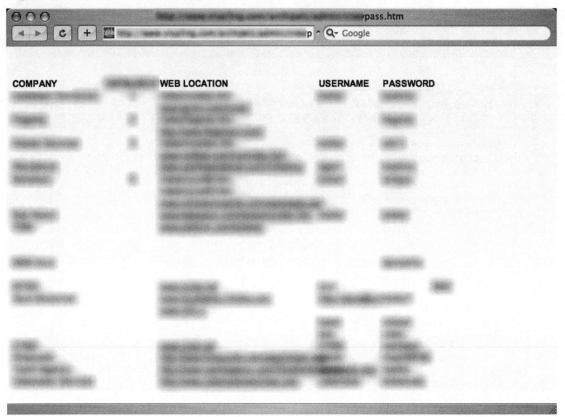

This document lists usernames and passwords for various websites. The document was stored on a website, presumably to allow the owner easy remote access to it. However, at some point the document's location was made public, and Google dutifully crawled it. Remember, public websites are generally just that—public. Don't combine public and private data without a great deal of forethought.

Police Reports

From what I understand, most police records are a matter of public record. So it doesn't surprise me when I see police reports like the one shown in Figure 6.62.

Figure 6.62 Police Reports Are Public Record. Okay

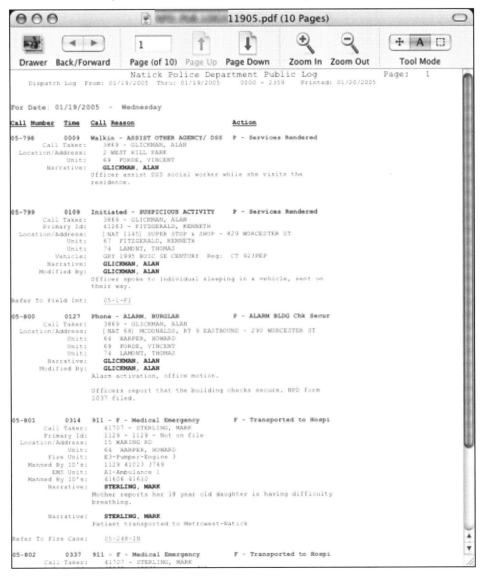

However, when I find a police report like the one shown in Figure 6.63, I begin to question the sanity of posting unfiltered police records.

Figure 6.63 That Means Your Victoria's Secret Account Info Is Too

This police report records the details of a theft of a woman's purse. The problem is that the contents of the woman's purse are listed in great detail, including the account number of her Victoria's Secret card! This is not the only occurrence of such a detailed police report found on the web. Figure 6.64 shows another more revealing report.

Figure 6.64 Robbed Twice, Thanks To Open Police Reports

This report details another petty theft, this time listing the account numbers of the Visa and MasterCard credit cards that were stolen. It's very likely that the cards were cancelled immediately after they were reported stolen, but the police report shown in Figure 6.65 lists personal numbers that are not as easy to replace.

Figure 6.65 Police Report Triple Robbery or "Mom, I have bad news"

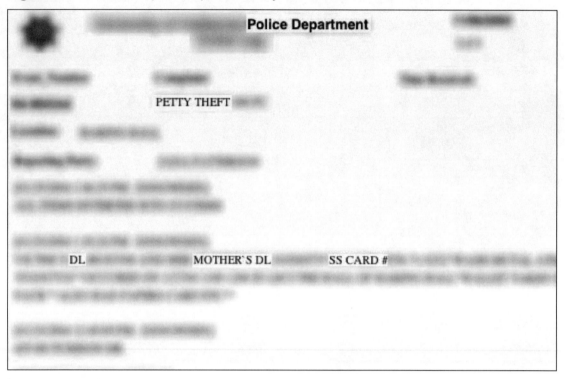

In this case, not only is the victim's driver's license number posted, but their social security number is listed alongside their mother's driver's license number—all of this posted on a public website, ripe for an identity thief's picking.[1]

---

[1] We're obviously in tricky water here, as these are dangerous searches indeed. All identifying information in these and following searches has been blurred out, and any information that could lead to the recreation of the Google query has been removed as well. Additionally, most of the sensitive documents found in this chapter have since been removed from the web.

Social Security Numbers

The Social Security Number (SSN) is the most sensitive piece of information a United States citizen possesses. Even an inexperienced criminal can use a pilfered SSN to establish a bank account, open a line of credit or more—all under the victim's name. In this section, we'll take a look at some of the ways an individual's SSN may end up online. Be advised that like the other sensitive searches in this book, every effort has been taken to obfuscate the selected documents and obscure the Google search that was used to locate them.

In most educational facilities, it is common to assign an identification number to students in order to keep their grades and personal information private. However, as shown in Figure 6.66, the identification number most often used is the student's social security number.

Figure 6.66 Social Security Numbers as Student ID Numbers

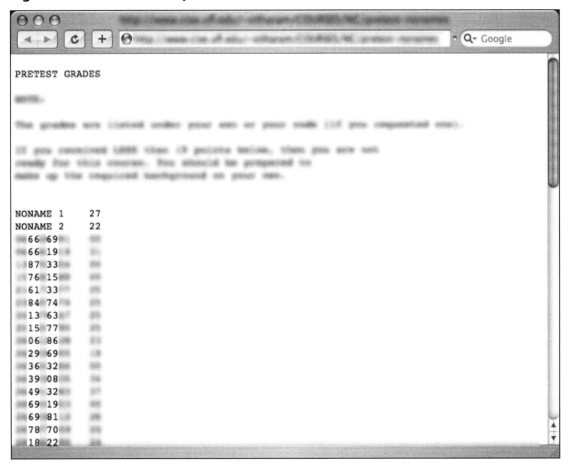

The SSN by itself is not necessarily a big deal, and when posted alongside student's grades (as shown in Figure 6.67) the system works well to keep student's progress private.

Figure 6.67 "Anonymous" Student Numbers and Grade Postings

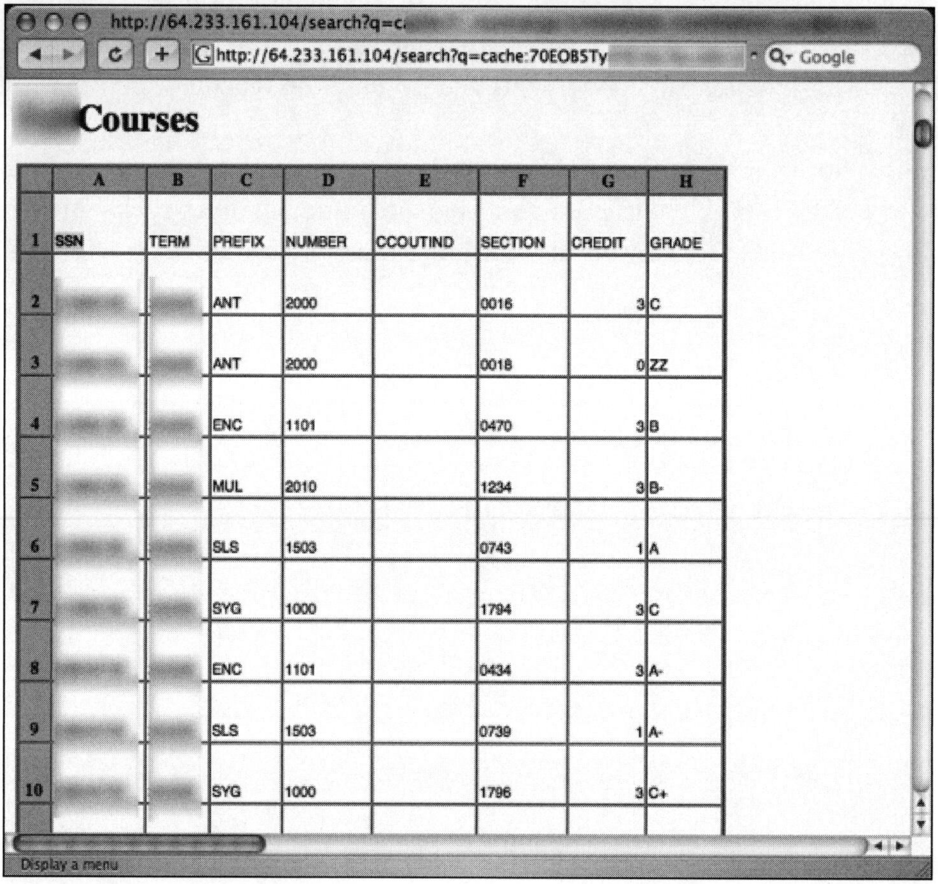

However, in many cases, student's names are posted right alongside their Social Security Number, as shown in Figure 6.68. This of course destroys the anonymity gained by using an identification number instead of a name.

Figure 6.68 Names and Social Security Numbers Together Again

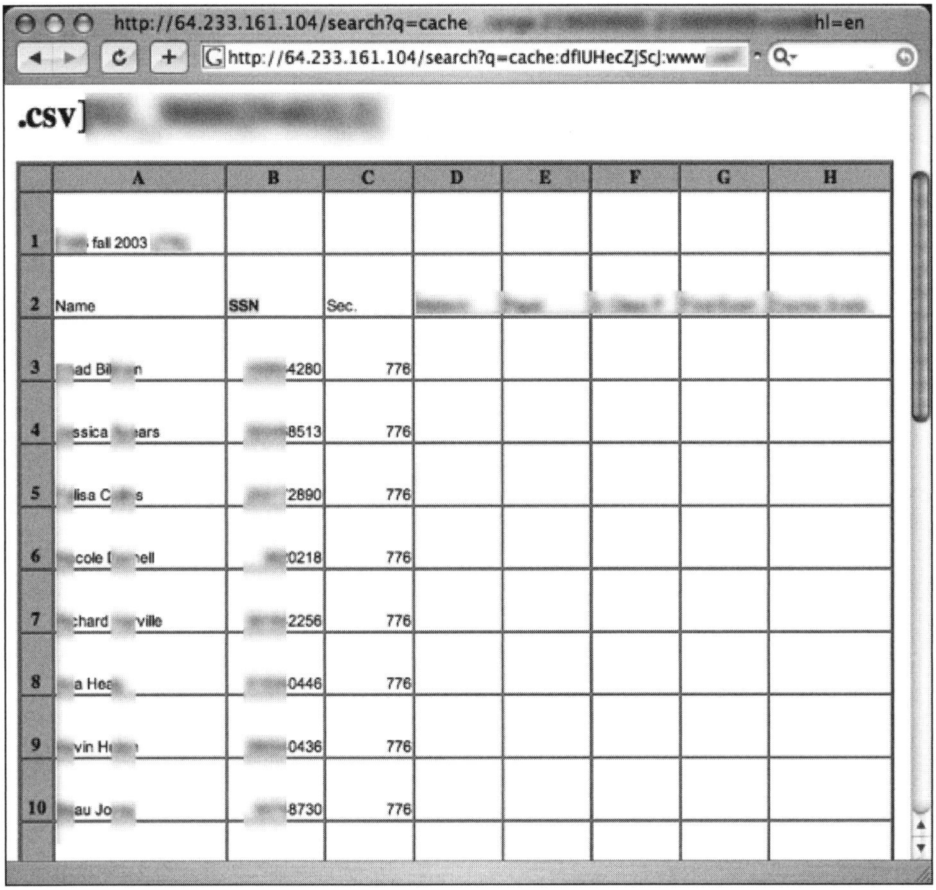

In some cases, these documents are not intended for public viewing, but somehow end up on Internet-facing websites. This is, of course, an unsafe handling practice and the documents end up in Google's cache. The document shown in Figure 6.69 was discovered sitting in an open directory by an anonymous Google hacker. Notice that it lists student's names, SSN and more. To make matters worse, this document was found on a US Government training facility website. The document has since been removed.

Figure 6.69 SSN and Names, an ID Thief's Birthday Present

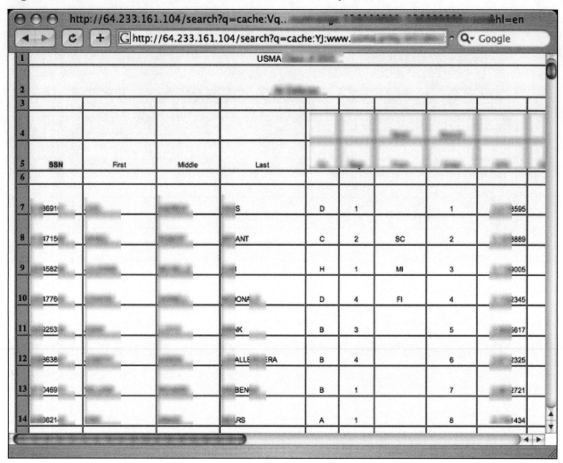

Social Security numbers appear on the web in other ways, most notably through user ignorance. The resume request shown in Figure 6.70 lists an individual's SSN in a message group post.

Figure 6.70 Hire This Guy. Here's His SSN

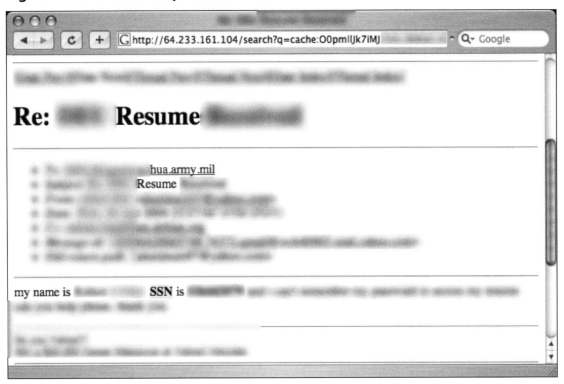

The document shown in Figure 6.71 is known as curriculum vitae, or a CV. I wasn't sure what a CV was, but after a bit of research I discovered it is a sort of résumé for really smart people.

Figure 6.71 I'm Smart. Want to See My CV?

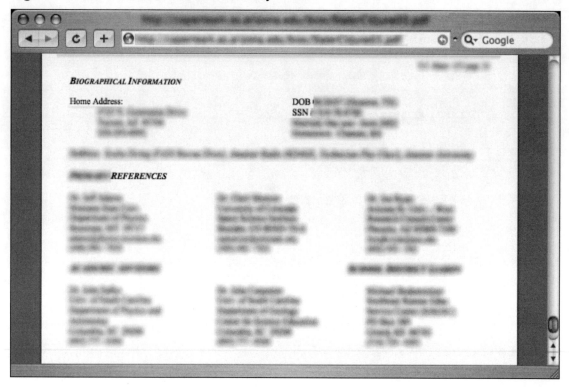

As for me, I think I'll keep my plain old résumé, especially if maintaining a CV means that I have to publicly expose my birthday and social security number. Finally, check out the spreadsheet shown in Figure 6.72 which lists the name, date of birth, sex, date of hire and SSN of a company's employees.

Figure 6.72 Employee Out Of the Closet Day

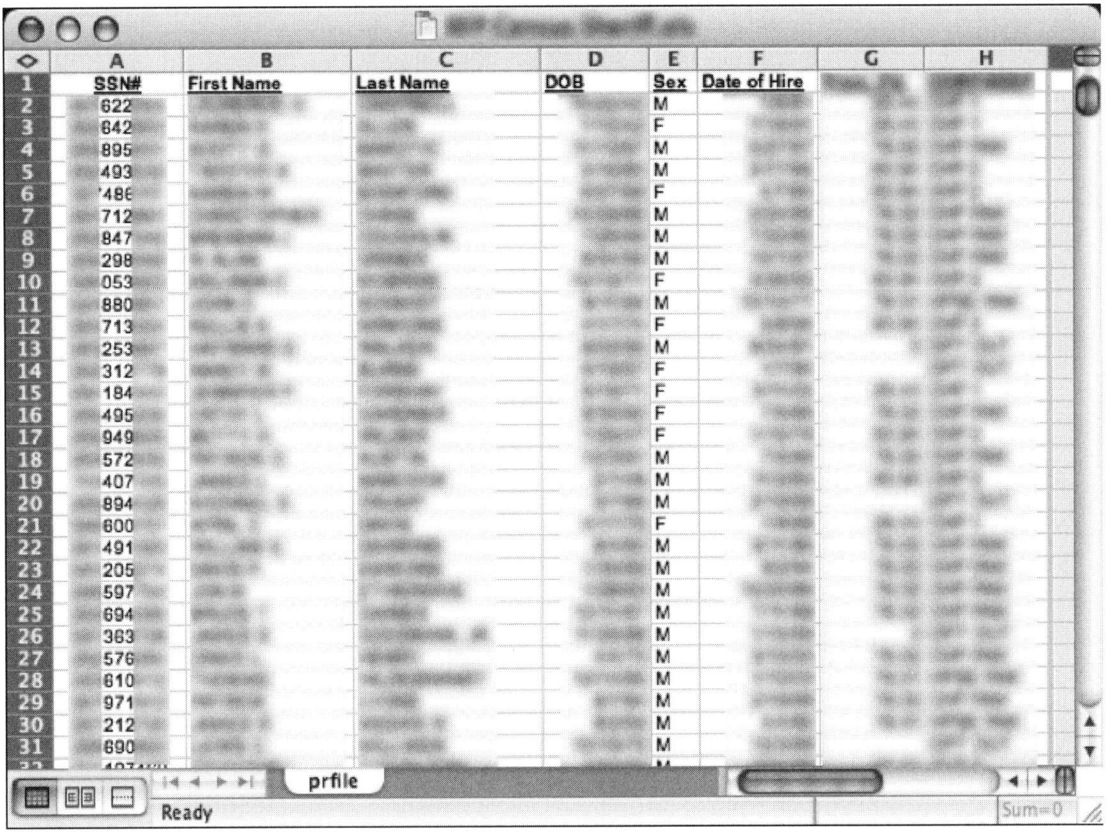

Credit Card Information

Credit card numbers are obviously very valuable, and should be kept well protected. However, as we'll see in this section, those numbers can be found on the web with very little effort. Figure 6.73 shows a relatively small document that lists a Visa credit card number alongside the associated expiration date.

Figure 6.73 Google Hacking Credit Card Info

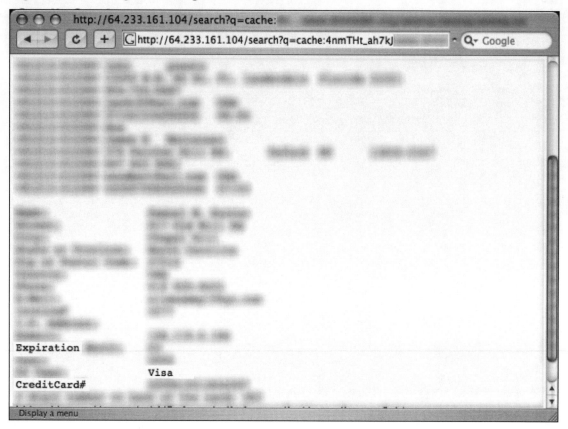

Figure 6.74 shows a larger document that lists no only credit card numbers and their associated expiration dates, but also the card certification value (CVV) number which is often used to validate that the card is in the hands of a legitimate bearer.

Figure 6.74 Google Hacking More Credit Card Info

Figure 6.75 shows an extremely large document that contains hundreds of bits of personal information about victims including name, address, phone numbers, credit card information, CVV codes and expiration dates.

Figure 6.75 Google Hacking Lots of Credit Card Info

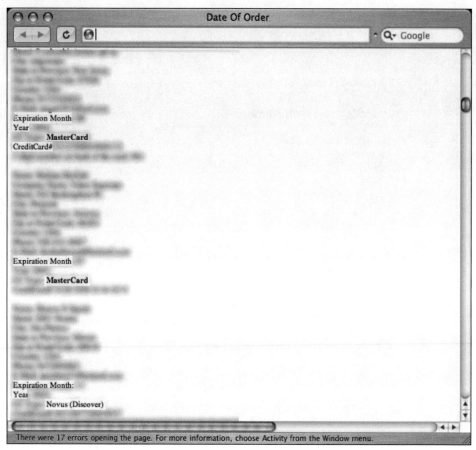

However, credit card numbers and expiration dates aren't the only financially sensitive bits of information on the web, as shown in Figure 6.76.

How Does this Stuff Get on the Web?

Most often, information like this is collected by *phishers* – criminals using electronic communication to solicit personal information—and kept in an online list or database. In many cases, investigators locate these lists or databases and post links to them in online discussion groups. When Google's crawlers follow the link, the captured data is exposed to Google Hackers. In other cases, carders (credit card number traders) post this data on the web in open-air web discussions, which Google then crawls and caches. For more information about phishing, see *Phishing Exposed* from Syngress Publishing.

Figure 6.76 Is Nothing Sacred?

These samples were collected from various web sites, and include bank routing numbers, PayPal usernames and passwords, eBay usernames and passwords, bank account and routing numbers and more, most likely collected by phishers.

Beyond Google

In some cases, Google is the first step in a longer hacking chain. Decent hackers will often take the next step beyond Google. In this section, we'll take a quick look at some interesting Google hacks that took an extra few steps to pull off. Still simple in execution, these examples show the creative lengths hackers will go to.

This first screenshot, shown in Figure 6.77 (submitted by CP) reports that a staff directory has been removed from the web for privacy purposes.

Figure 6.77 Staff Contact List Removed?

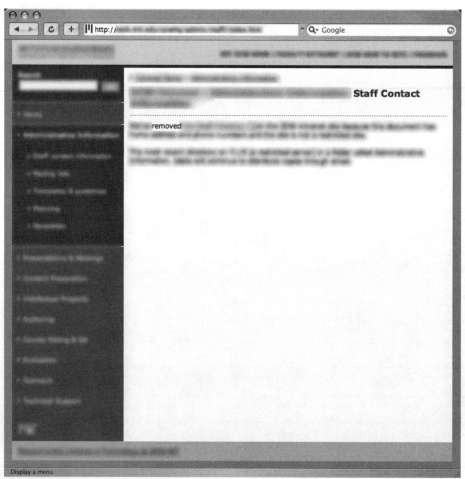

This isn't a bad idea, but the problem is that the old document must also be removed from the website, or sites like archive.org will hold onto the document's link indefinitely. Figure 6.78 shows the staff contact document pulled from the original website, thanks to a link from archive.org.

Figure 6.78 Staff Contact List Recovered

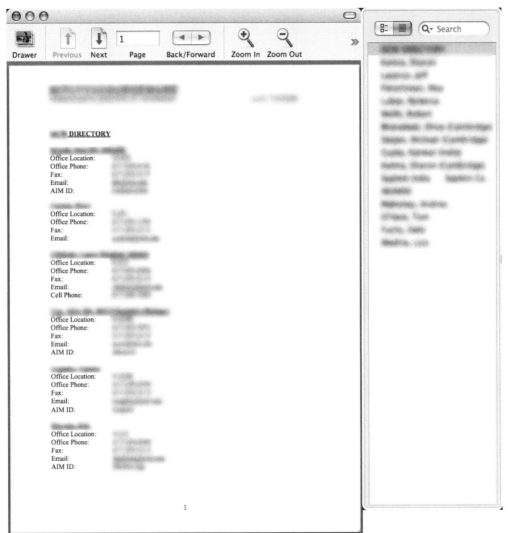

In this next example, a Google hacker noticed a password reference sitting in a PDF document, as shown in Figure 6.79.

Figure 6.79 A PDF File Password Reference

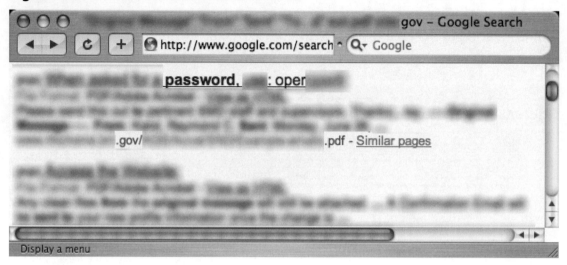

When downloaded, the PDF file does indeed contain a password reference. In this case, it comes in the form of a link to a password-protected PDF document as shown in Figure 6.80.

Figure 6.80 A Link to a Protected Document, And the Associated Password

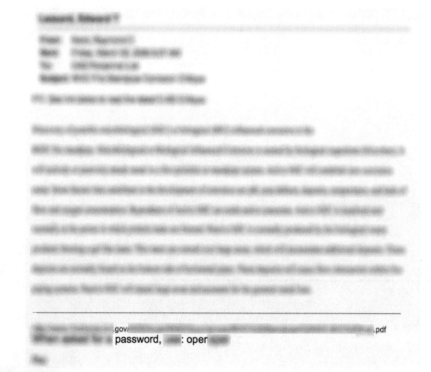

As seen in Figure 6.81, the referenced PDF file is indeed password protected.

Figure 6.81 Password Protected PDF Document

Entering the password opens the document, as shown in Figure 6.82.

Figure 6.82 Sensitive Document Open with Pilfered Password

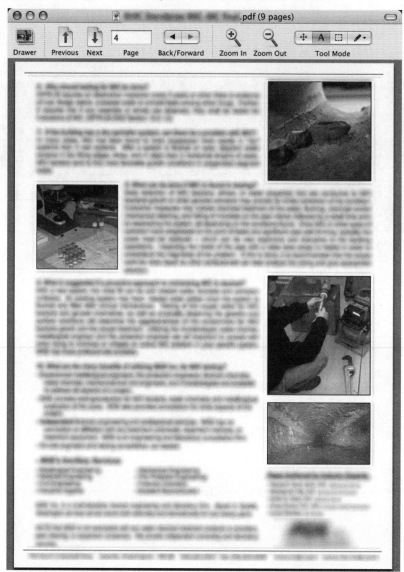

It makes no sense to password-protect a document then give out the password, but in this case the problem occurred because the original document containing the password reference was not meant to be public. In this case, the blunder lead to the revelation of a sensitive Government document.

Summary

This chapter is all about what can go drastically wrong when the Google hacking threat is ignored. Use this chapter whenever you have trouble conveying the seriousness of the threat. Help spread the word, and become part of the solution and not part of the problem. And before you go sending cease and desist papers to Google, remember— it's not Google's fault if your sensitive data makes it online.

Chapter 7

P2P Hacking

As we continue our pause from strict no-tech hacking, we'll cover another low-tech skill: peer-to-peer (P2P) hacking. In keeping with the spirit of no-tech, let's assume a guy has no budget, no commercial hacking software, no support from organized crime and no fancy gear. In fact, let's even take away Google. With all those restrictions, is this guy still a threat to you? Have a look at this chapter and judge for yourself.

Understanding P2P Hacking

A peer-to peer (P2P) network is composed of a number of clients (called peers) who want to share files or data. Most often, peer-to-peer networks carry audio, video or program files shared by users who join the network. The workings of a P2P network are beyond the scope of this book, but for our purposes, let's just say that P2P is one of the most common file sharing services in existence. In order to join a P2P network, you simply download a P2P client (such as Acquisition for the Mac, shown below), run it and begin searching for files to download.

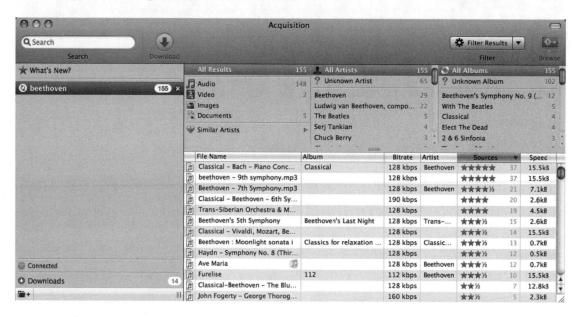

A search for *Beethoven*, like the one above "magically" returns a list of files other P2P users have shared that contain the word *Beethoven*. Results are typically sorted by popularity. In the example above, the top three results include a piano concerto by Bach (mistakenly listed as being by Beethoven), and Beethoven's 7th and 9th symphonies. This brings up an interesting point—shared files on P2P networks are not always what they appear to be. A Bach concerto listed as being performed by Beethoven is a fairly benign example, but since any user can share any kind of file, the concerto could just as easily be anything: a movie about mayo, a picture of a pickle, or a file containing a computer virus. A malicious user could easily share any kind of nasty file. B the malicious files don't interest me as much as the files shared accidentally.

As no-tech hackers already know, there are thousands of Internet users who have downloaded and installed P2P software and have accidentally shared sensitive files.

Gaining access to these files is as easy as installing a P2P client and submitting creative searches. In this chapter, we'll take a look at some of the files I've found floating around various peer-to-peer networks.

We'll start with some basics and work our way up to some really interesting stuff. The next photo shows a relatively simple-looking Word document that lists a company's corporate clients.

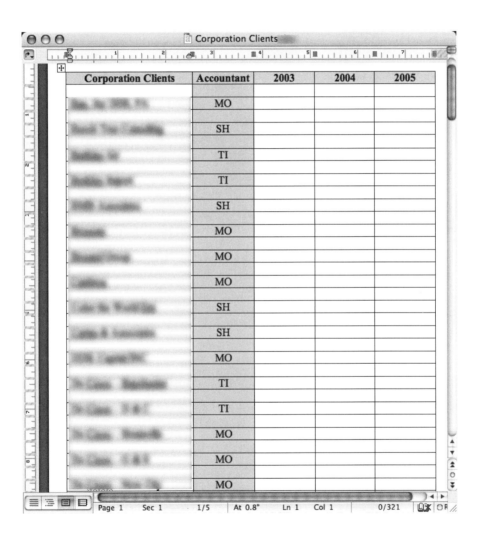

The quality of this next photo is awful, but I'll present it as I found it. I think it's a screen printout that was scanned in as an image. Hopefully it's not what it looks like—a photo that was printed in a newspaper.

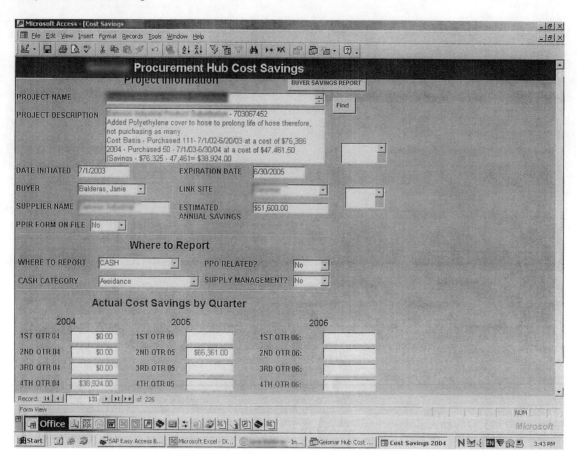

However the photo came into being, it reveals an awful lot of information. The task bar at the bottom is a shoulder surfer's dream, but the Access database screen is a goldmine of information. The screen shows a cost savings report for a large company that lists very specific details about a project, including expenses and annual cost savings. The information is extremely dated, but based on the recognizable name of the company; someone would certainly be interested in more info just like it.

Find One, Search More

Once you find an interesting document, it's simple to find more from the same computer. Most P2P clients allow you to browse all the shared files on a P2P user's computer. If an attacker finds one marginally sensitive document, he'll almost certainly browse the machine that shared the file to find more. Although his search will only be limited to the files that user is sharing, if the user's sharing one sensitive document, he's almost certainly sharing others.

The next photo shows a customer invoice.

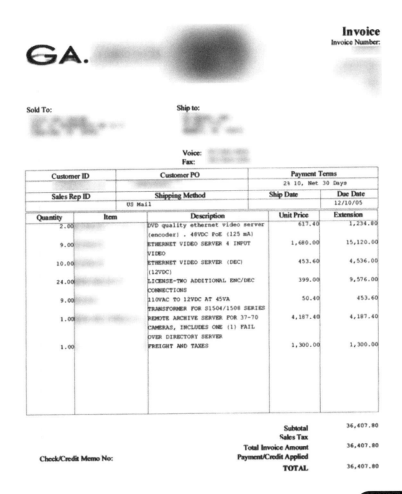

This invoice is dated as well, but it reveals client information and pricing data. The most interesting thing to me is that the invoice lists item descriptions, which seem to layout a very high-end security system. It lists video servers (capable of supporting up to forty cameras), video encoders, power supplies and more. It seems ironic that the invoice for this high-tech security system would be sitting out on a P2P network for the world to see.

Here's another interesting document: a cellular phone bill.

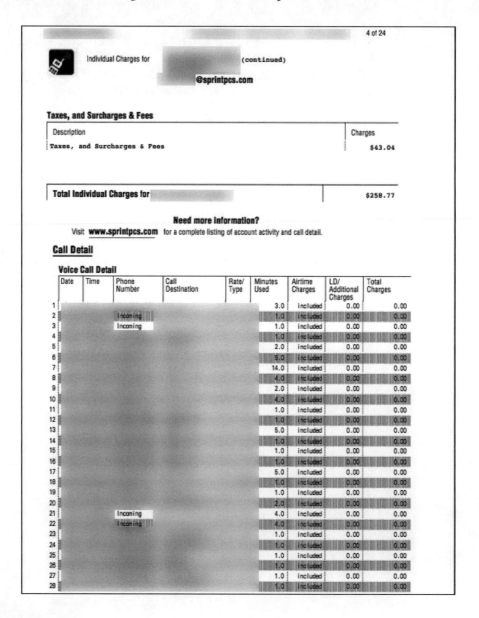

I don't personally think I'd want to share this info with the world. The 24-page document lists the customer's name, address and phone number and goes on to list an entire month's cellular phone history. It lists every call placed and every call received. It goes on to list the time, duration and charge of a month's worth of calls. If a high-tech hacker were to try to gain access to this data electronically, it would be a difficult task. But for a no-tech hacker, it only takes a quick P2P hacking session or a round of dumpster diving.

What If a Hacker Is after Me?

It's scary to think about a hacker targeting your personal information, but understand that P2P hacking is not about targeting specific individuals. P2P hacking is about finding interesting information based on specific keywords. If a hacker's after you, he or she is probably not going to log into a P2P client in search of your information because this makes the assumption that you're running a P2P client *and* that you have shared personal data there. Both of these are rather wild assumptions. So if you do run P2P software, make sure you know exactly what it is you are sharing, and then focus your attention on making sure your personal firewall, and anti-virus/spyware/adware software is current and correctly configured.

Word documents abound on P2P networks, and may are great sources of personal information. The document below lists more info than most.

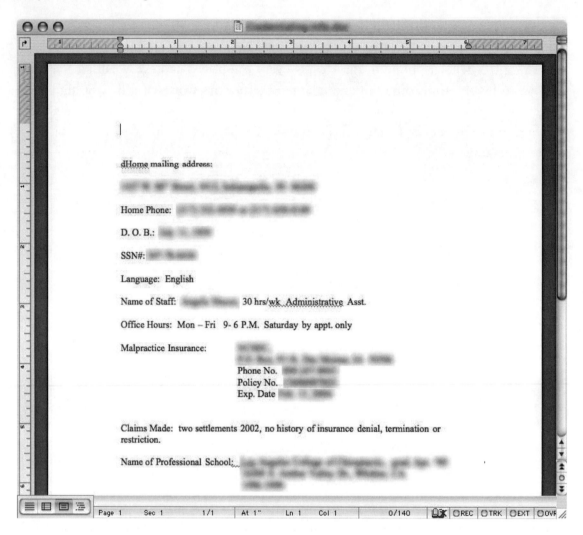

The name, date of birth and social security number are interesting bits of information, but this document reveals insurance policy information as well. This all pales in comparison to financial information. Take a look at the document below.

Attach your Schedule 1 (federal tax), and Form 428 (provincial or territorial tax) here. Also attach here any other schedules, information slips, forms, receipts, and documents that you need to include with your return.

Net Income

Enter your **total income** from line 150				150	53,331 40

Pension adjustment (box 52 on T4, box 34 on all T4A slips)	206	1,396 00			
Registered pension plan deduction (box 20 on all T4 slips and box 32 on all T4A slips)			207	550 38	
RRSP deduction (see Schedule 7; attach receipts)			208	1,420 76	
Saskatchewan Pension Plan deduction	(maximum $600)		209		
Annual union, professional, or like dues (box 44 on all T4 slips and receipts)			212	950 90	
Child care expenses (attach Form T778)			214		
Attendant care expenses			215		
Business investment loss Gross	228	Allowable deduction	217		
Moving expenses			219		
Support payments made Total	230	Allowable deduction	220		
Carrying charges and interest expenses (attach Schedule 4)			221		
Deduction for CPP or QPP contributions on self-employment and other earnings (attach Schedule 8)			222		
Exploration and development expenses (attach Form T1229)			224		
Other employment expenses			229		
Clergy residence deduction			231		
Other deductions Specify:			232		
	Add lines 207 to 224, 229, 231, and 232.	233	2,922 04		2,922 04
	Line 150 minus line 233. This is your **net income before adjustments.**	234			50,409 36
Social benefits repayment (if you reported income on line 113, 119, or 146, see Help)			235		
	Line 234 minus line 235 (if negative, enter "0"). If you have a spouse or common-law partner, see **Help.** This is your **net income.**	236			50,409 36

This tax document was most likely part of a computer-based tax preparation program. It provides a summary of this individual's financial information. Even more financial information can be found in documents like the one below, which really caught my eye because of the words *direct debit* in the header.

Please confirm your Direct Debit details

Please confirm that your payment details are correct, then place your order. If you've made any errors when typing in your information, you can still go back and correct them.

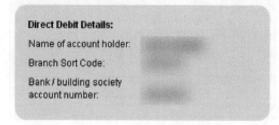

Direct Debit Details:

Name of account holder:

Branch Sort Code:

Bank / building society
account number:

The company name that will appear on your bank statement against the direct debit will be Wanadoo.

The Direct Debit Guarantee:
The Direct Debit Guarantee is offered by all banks and building societies that take part in the Direct Debit scheme. The efficiency and security of the scheme is monitored and protected by your own bank or building society.

If the amounts to be paid or if the payment dates change Wanadoo will notify you 10 working days in advance of your account being debited or as otherwise agreed.

If an error is made by _____ or your bank or building society, you are guaranteed a full and immediate refund from your branch of the amount paid.

You can cancel a Direct Debit at any time by writing to your bank or building society. Please also send a copy of your letter to us.

The owner of this document first viewed it in his or her browser, and then probably saved it as a file on the local hard drive. Unfortunately, it was saved into a directory that peer-to-peer software used as a share folder, and the saved document was shared to the world. Unfortunately for this user, his name, bank account number and branch code are now a matter of public record.

Other bank information is easy to come by also as shown in the next photo.

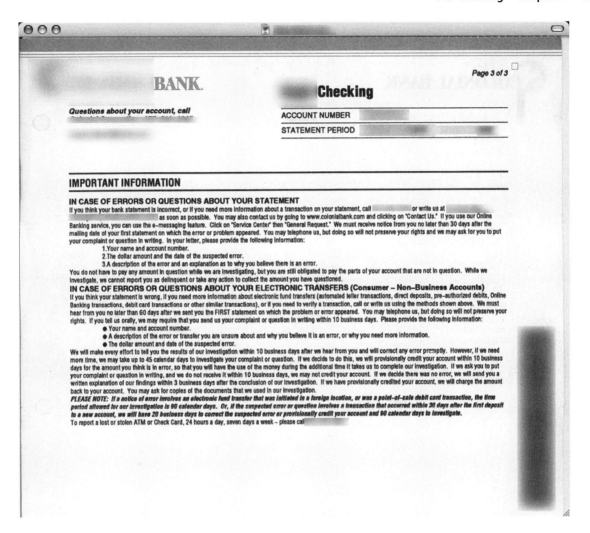

This multi-page document lists account information including account number, balances, charges and withdrawals. Page after page of the document are included in the report as shown below.

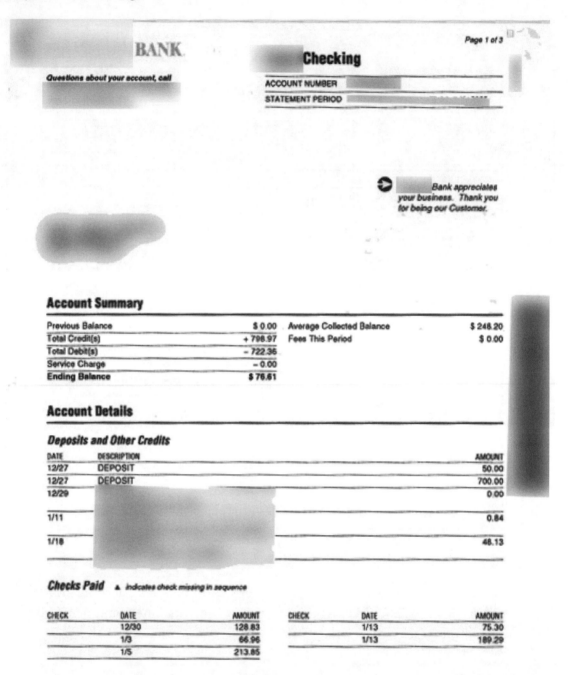

This is great stuff for a no-tech hacker, but it only describes a single account. Documents like the one below list information about multiple accounts. Now we're getting into some really crazy stuff.

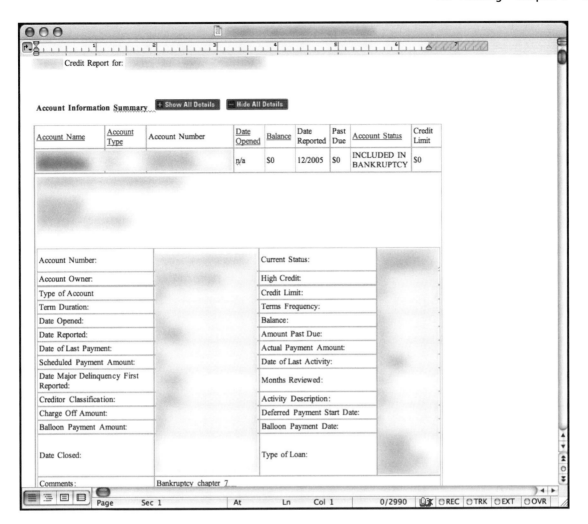

This is a full-blown credit report. It lists account names, bank information, balances, loans and more—just about every bit of financial information a person can accumulate. Identity thieves need much less information than this to completely take over a person's identity. Unfortunately, as the next capture shows, there is no shortage of this kind of information available.

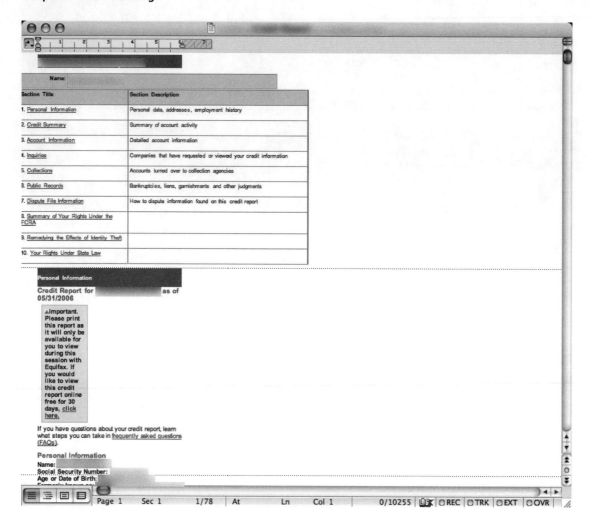

I could list hundreds of these things, but let's take a look at one more. Check out the next report.

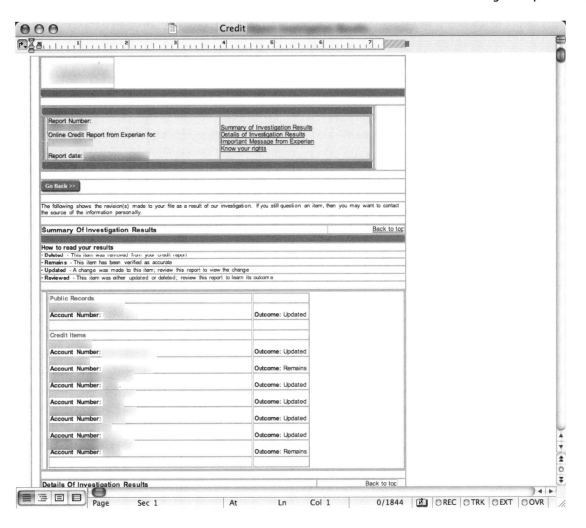

Other simpler documents, like the one below, just list the sensitive bits. It's like credit-report-concentrate (no pulp).

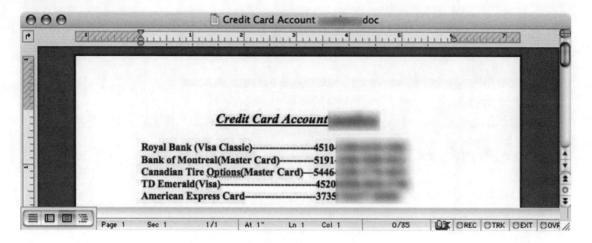

I could go on and on, but there's really no need. There's no shortage of sensitive information on P2P networks, and it doesn't take much skill at all to find it. Let's take a look at a real-world P2P hacking session.

Real World P2P Hacking:
The Case of the Naughty Chiropractor

When I found the document below, I distinctly remember thinking "how cute." It's not really an interesting document—it simply welcomes new chiropractic patients, and goes on a bit about how important muscles and spines and stuff really are.

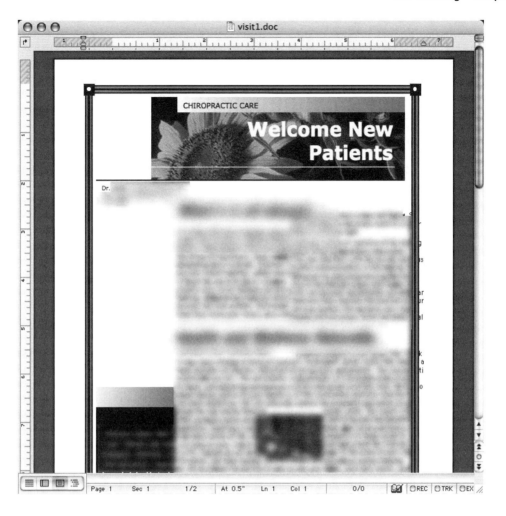

But after thinking about it a moment, I began to wonder if I had stumbled on to a doctor's home PC. I right-clicked the file in my P2P client, and selected *Browse* to see other files on that computer. The results are shown in the next photo.

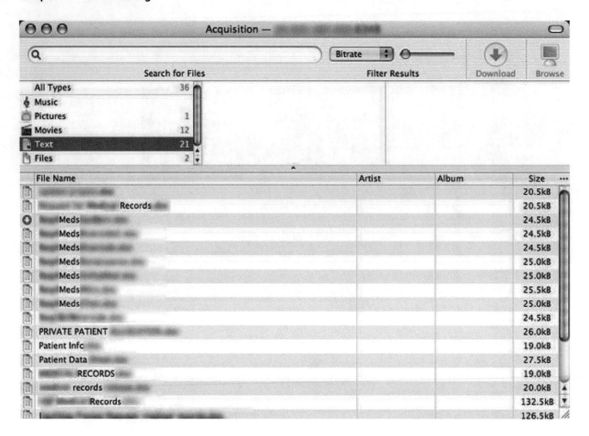

I clicked the *Text* link to see text-based files, such as Microsoft Word documents, and as the results scrolled down the screen, I could hardly believe my eyes. I saw file after file of records, private patient data, and meds (medication) requests. I was looking at private patient data. I was scrolling through a list of documents that contained some extremely sensitive patient medical data, and there was a good chance that others in the P2P network had already downloaded these documents. There was no telling where in the world this data had already traveled. This info made me realize that this probably wasn't a personal machine—it was most likely the machine the doctor used for business. I decided to browse the machine a bit more. I clicked the *Movies* link at the top of the P2P screen and glanced through the results, shown in the next screen.

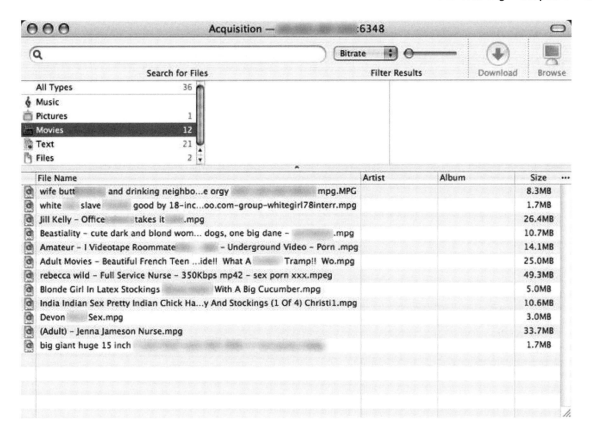

The names of the videos were so foul that I instinctively looked over my shoulder to see if anyone was seeing what I was seeing. Most of the pornographic videos centered on sexy nurses, teenage girls and women in stockings. Some of the video titles were so disgusting I had to blur out the majority of the title to even present the photo. The most disturbing videos described sex acts with animals and mentioned terms like "white slave." The videos were nasty enough, but then I remembered this was most likely a doctor's machine. If this was the doctor's machine, I wondered if his patients had any idea that he was not only completely irresponsible with their records, but that he was a complete sleaze to boot. I know I wouldn't want a doctor that collected this kind of stuff touching anyone I cared about.

I flipped back to the *Text* list, and read the name of a file that did not seem sensitive in nature. I downloaded the file, shown in the next photo.

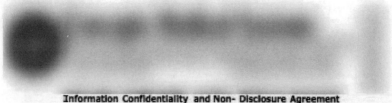

Information Confidentiality and Non- Disclosure Agreement

I understand state and federal laws prohibit the release of any information related to patients without specific signed consent designed for the release of medical information.

I _____, will:
(Print Your Full Name)

1. Always maintain an awareness of people within viewing distance when transcribing patient medical information. I will likewise, use caution when handling documents that bear patient medical information by not leaving the information open for public view.

2. Disclose this information solely to individuals who have signed a non-disclosure agreement with, or who have expressed written approval from ▮▮▮▮▮▮▮▮▮▮▮ to receive information.

3. Not make any contact nor agreement with anyone without written and/or verbal consent from ▮▮▮▮ or its authorized staff on any idea submitted without approval.

4. I agree not to use, directly or indirectly, any such information provided by ▮▮▮▮ for my own benefit of any person, firm, or corporation.

5. All subcontractors and affiliates of this company have a moral, professional and legal obligation to protect the confidentiality of patient, physician, employee and administrative information. It is the obligation of the employee/subcontractor to maintain confidentiality while on and off duty. This obligation continues even after the termination of the employment relationship has ended.

6. This agreement supersedes all previous agreements, written or oral, relating to the above subject matter and shall not be changed orally.

Acknowledgment of Confidentiality Policy

I herby acknowledge that I have been informed of State and Federal Laws relating to the protection of patient medical information. I understand the penalties for unauthorized release of this information. I have had an opportunity to ask and receive answers to questions regarding this confidence policy.

_____   _____
Signature   Date

The document wasn't meant to be funny, but it made me laugh nonetheless. It was a non-disclosure agreement that the doctor's employees were to sign and date, agreeing that they would not release patient information without a signed consent. It went on to state that employees had certain moral and professional obligations to protect patient confidentiality, and that there are penalties for the unauthorized release of patient information. I couldn't believe that this document was sitting in the same folder as private patient data and hot nurse porn. But no-tech hackers see all sorts of interesting things.

Chapter 8

People Watching

Scott Pinzon, my friend and this book's technical editor, has always liked (and related to) that song, "The Girl from Ipanema." But the dude watching her in that song is clearly an amateur people-watcher. If he had read this chapter, he probably would have figured out what hotel she's staying at (hotel key card), her probable income (are those flip-flops from Wal-Mart or Dolce-Gabbana?), and maybe even her room number (after shoulder-surfing the waiter to catch a glimpse of the room number on her bill). Skilled people watchers can learn a whole lot more in just a few quick glances. In this chapter we'll take a look at a few examples of the types of things that draws a no-tech hacker's eye.

How to "People Watch"

People watching is a real skill. There's so much to it, that I can't possibly cover all the angles in one short chapter. But it's an important topic, because a decent no-tech hacker can get a good read on a person by just paying attention. In this chapter, we'll take a look at a few simple examples of effective people watching.

Let's start with the gentleman in the next photo—the guy in the foreground with the baseball cap. What can you tell me about him?

Let's start with the boots. Although I'm not well-versed enough to know an Adidas GSG9 from a High Tech Magnum Stealth, I can say without a doubt that those are tactical boots. The jeans are pretty non-descript, except for the fact that his wallet's sticking out of them (no, I'm not tempted to snag it to get a better profile on the guy), and his black T-shirt tells me that he's a tough-guy type (or a severe wanna-be). His gaze is locked on a female flight attendant, which seconds the tough-guy image and lets us in on his sexual preference. His haircut is short, although it's too soon to tell if he'd describe it as "high and tight"—a military term for hair that's cut high... and tight. His glasses are Oakleys, and I've heard people call them *shooters*, because they're often found at gun ranges, worn by people who shoot. You know, guns. Topping all this off is the baseball hat. There's a logo on the back that's hard to read, but here's a close-up.

The logo reads *BenelliUSA.com*. Here's a screen shot of a Benelli USA web page.

Saying Benelli makes guns is like saying NASA makes bottle rockets. Benelli makes serious camouflaged armor-piercing shotguns with, like, built-in missile launchers and flamethrowers. OK, so they don't make missile launchers and flamethrowers, but they make serious weapons for hunters and Marines and cops. Take a guess which of the three this guy is. Think you've got it nailed? I'd say this guy is either law enforcement or military—most likely Special Forces of some kind. Now, let's say, hypothetically, that he pre-boarded the plane, in front of a little old lady in a wheelchair? Would that change your perception of this guy? It would change mine.

Let's take a look at another example. Check out the next photo.

This one's pretty easy. Let's take a quick inventory. Hair: high and tight. Arms: muscular and tan (below the elbows). Accessories: one wedding band and an Iron Man watch. The first impression is simple—married, and military.

A quick shoulder surf confirms this. His current email subject is "United States Military Casualty Statistics," and his inbox shows emails from Lieutenant Colonels (LTC) and Majors (MAJ). I don't really care what this guy's up to because I'm not one of the bad guys. However, if I were a bad guy, I'd have access to a lot of information about this guy in a very short period of time.

Let's do one more. Check out the next photo.

Using the rotating lens on my camera, I stood with my back to this guy and took the shot backwards. In the process, I caught a bit of my shirt in the shot, which blurred the edges of the photo. But taking a look at our target, we see pressed slacks, black socks and wing tips. His shirt is decidedly business casual, although it's a strange kind of pinkish orange. He's wearing a nice watch and he's sporting a big class ring. The magazine is some sort of financial/news rag.

So far, he seems to fit the mold of a managerial type, but there's more to the story. Moving in closer, I stood next to him and took a photo of his bag, shown in the next picture.

The guy didn't seem to notice that I stood right next to him and took pictures of his stuff. The bag sported the logo of a very specific U.S. Government agency which had recently been highlighted in the international news scene. Because of the agency's very specific mission and recent public interest, I knew somewhere in the world someone would be very interested to know where this guy was headed and where he was from. I walked back to my original position some distance ahead of him, and lined up my next backwards shot.

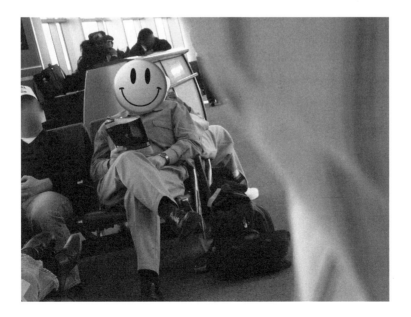

I didn't know it at the time, but he looked right into my lens as I took the photo and gave me this look. I really wish I could show you the look on his face, but I won't jeopardize his privacy. Just believe me when I say he gave me this dead serious *why are you taking my picture, you stalking terrorist scumbag* kind of look. Had I known he was looking right at my camera when I took the photo, I definitely wouldn't have hung around long enough to get this next photo that captures his name and frequent flier number.

The thing that surprises me the most about this example is that I know this guy saw me take his picture. There's a good chance he saw me take quite a few pictures, and he may have even watched me as I moved around him getting (what I thought were) relatively discrete photos of him and his gear. Knowing that he worked for an *interesting* government agency, I'm not sure why he didn't do something about me. I don't have any ill intent, but there's no way he could have know that. For all he knew, I could have been some kind of creepy stalker taking photos of him at the airport, or worse. I could have been sponsored by a foreign government, who tasked me with the job of tracking his agency's activities. There's really no telling who I was, but this guy chose to do what most people do—absolutely nothing. Therein lies the problem. At some point creepy stalker people should be reported to *someone*. I can only hope that the worst thing that happens to this guy is he gets his blurred, unrecognizable photo published in this humble book.

Play It Smart

You might be proud of the company you work for, but sometimes flying the team colors is a bad idea. These examples focused on individuals in the Government and Military. I'm not trying to make any kind of statement, it's just that I didn't happen to include any corporate examples despite having examples from the entire corporate spectrum: banking, finance, manufacturing, investing, healthcare, retail and more. Depending on current events, political climate or other factors, anyone can become a target of public scrutiny or unwanted attention. Government agencies have requested for years that employees travel low profile, but those same agencies still produce signature items sporting the agency logo. The best advice I can offer you is to play it smart. Take a moment to consider your profile, and every now and then play it paranoid. A no-tech hacker might be the least of your worries.

Chapter 9

Kiosks

Those self-serve electronic terminals are everywhere. They sit there all smug, taunting no-tech hackers, just begging to be messed with. And guess what no-tech hackers do? Well most of the time, they just look at them. But as you already know, hackers don't see things the way normal people do. When a hacker looks at a kiosk, the thing opens up, exposing more than you would ever imagine. But what happens when the kiosk is more than a kiosk? What happens when the kiosk holds airline passenger information? What if the kiosk holds confidential patient information? What if the kiosk holds cash? Do no-tech hackers approach these devices any differently? Probably not. After all, the no-touch approach goes a long way. But if a no-tech hacker actually decides to touch one of these things, life gets really interesting. Then, they might do something really wicked, like hit SHIFT and break into the thing.

Understanding Kiosk Hacking

"An Interactive kiosk is a computer terminal that provides information access via electronic methods. Interactive kiosks sometimes resemble telephone booths, but can also be used while sitting on a bench or chair." *http://en.wikipedia.org/wiki/Internet_kiosk.*

Kiosks are appearing everywhere these days. No one realizes this more than a hacker. Although most people don't view interactive kiosks as a security threat, keep in mind that these are networked data terminals that connect to backend databases that store lots of interesting data: names, addresses, phone numbers, social security numbers, credit card data, bank information and even medical data. Although most hackers only poke at these devices because they're interesting, malicious no-tech hackers may be after more than a few laughs. Let's take a look at a few kiosks through the eyes of a no-tech hacker.

The next photo shows a typical airport self-check kiosk.

When I see a machine like this, I ask myself a few questions. I wonder what operating system the machine is running. Realizing that the thing is networked, I wonder about the type of protocols it uses, and if it's running TCP/IP, I wonder what addresses and ports it uses. After more than ten years of thinking of machines as addresses on a network, this is reflex. Finding the answers to these questions with traditional methods would require a fair amount of work.

First, I would need to find a place to jack into the kiosk's network. Then (assuming I figured out the network protocols the machine used) I would need to attach a machine to the network and start sniffing traffic to see what I could see. If the network was quiet, I would have to start scanning the network to try to get the machine to respond. Once the kiosk talked to me, I would analyze the results to guess the operating system. Once I had nailed all of this information down, I could form an attack plan. This would be a boring (I mean typical) approach. If I wanted to have more fun, I would attack the kiosk's inputs. Ignoring the on-screen keyboard (which certainly won't allow me to enter any interesting break characters) I would focus on the credit card swipes. I would probably burn some nasty one, two, or three-track "credit cards" and swipe them all through the reader to try to get the kiosk to gag. If I were feeling all über, I would make my own fake passports loaded with wicked data and swipe them through the reader to try to break the thing. In order to cover all the bases, I guess I could bring a big bag of faked cards and passports and pass them all through (while fending off the swarms of TSA agents) knowing that eventually something would bust. Then I would smirk from my federal holding cell, knowing that I was *this close* to owning an airport kiosk.

Or, I could go no-tech, and keep my eyes open as I went about my everyday—and perfectly legal—business. Then, just maybe, I'd see something like this.

I would walk up, all casual-like, and snap a few photos like this:

And then, I'd know that the kiosk ran some derivative of Windows because only DOS uses that ugly font, and DOS don't network so well, so this was either a command shell or a single-user mode. I'd know that it sat on a TCP/IP network and that the kiosk used an IP address of 10.160.7.26. I'd know this was a private network because of the reserved "10." address. I'd also know that the kiosk attached to a server at 10.52.20.4 and that it tried to connect on port 402, which IANA says is used by the *Genie protocol*, which is used by a product called Altiris. My friend Chris Eagle makes the next research step quite elegant—he suggests a "feeling lucky" Google search for *"Creating TCP socket for" "on 402"* which confirms that the kiosk is running Windows, that it is running Altiris software and that the error message is coming from *DOS BootWorks*. I'd know all this without touching the machine or the network and without risking any legal unpleasantness. This is how no-tech hackers operate.

A no-tech hacker already knows the lowdown on things like the public Internet phone in this next photo.

A no-tech hacker would know—simply by paying attention—that the high-tech phone ran *chkdisk* which hinted at it DOS roots, that it suffered from a bad hard drive and exactly which file record segments were bad on the poor device. He or she would know all of this because the next photo proves the silly thing coughed up a hairball.

Airport information screens are just as easy to read, especially when they throw errors. The next photo reveals a Windows task bar.

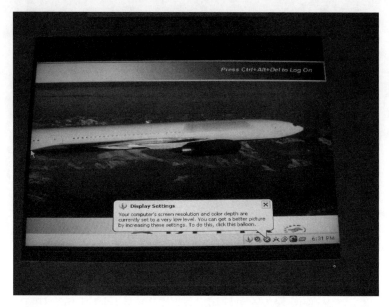

As we discuss in Chapter 3, each icon has meaning. We can tell (among other things) that the terminal runs Windows and that the airport relies on Symantec AntiVirus (fifth icon from the left).

Departure boards are equally open to a no-tech hacker's gaze, as the next photo shows.

This screen reveals information about the database that departure information is drawn from, the addresses and protocols that are in use, and even that the application is completely custom since a Google search for the various diagnostic messages reveals absolutely nothing.

Leaving airport terminals alone, let's take a look at a typical hospital. Even when they're in the hospital, no-tech hackers remain curious. Check out the next photo.

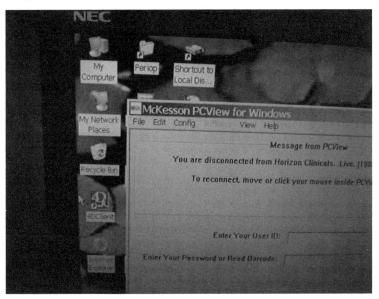

One look reveals the always-popular Windows operating system, and a couple of interesting applications: McKesson PCView (which returns a whopping six Google results) and *4dClient* (which smells strongly of Novell). The next photo helps complete the picture.

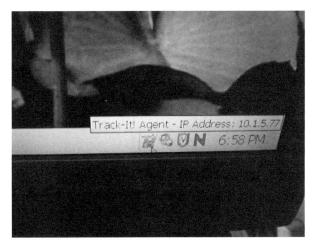

The big 'N' suggests a Novell Netware client, along with the McAfee antivirus icon, and the icon for Numara's *Track-It* help desk and asset management software. The IP address is also visible. I realize this seems like scanty information, but keep in mind that this is all captured without touching a keyboard and without leveraging any high-tech attack whatsoever. Each tiny bit of information is a freebie that a traditional attacker would have to work for.

The mobile nurse stations at the hospital are even cooler targets. Check it out in the next photo. It's mobile, wireless and irresistible.

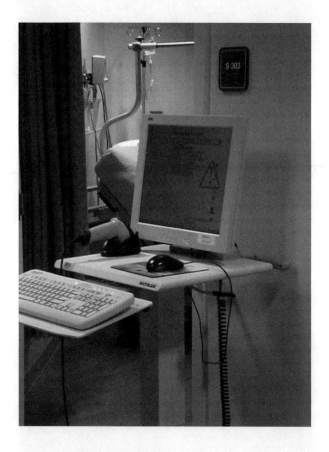

Even a far-off view shows that the machine's running Windows, and that Active Desktop is enabled. A closer view gets even more interesting.

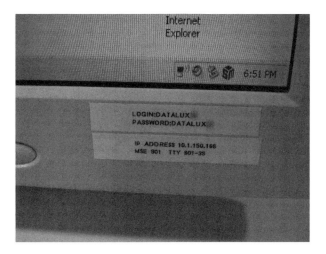

So, looking at the icons, I can tell that the machine's on a wireless network and that the machine's volume is not muted. Fun. I can see that the machine uses USB or PC cards, and that the time is 6:51PM. I can also tell that the IP address is 10.1.150.166 and that HOLY CRAP!!!1!1!1! IS THAT A PASSWORD?!? Yes, there on that sticker is a username and password to the hospital network. Let me type that out in italics for added effect. *A username and password to the hospital network.*

"But there can't be patient information on that thing," you might be saying. Take a look at the next photo.

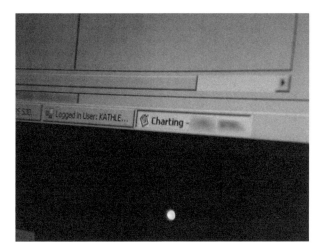

Yes, I blurred almost the entire picture, but that is the word *charting*, and yes, that's a patient's chart, chock full of all sorts of sensitive medical information. Can you spell HIPAA? I'm not sure this particular hospital can.

Standing around watching an interactive kiosk can get intensely boring. Eventually a no-tech hacker is going to want to get … *interactive* with the kiosk. There are a total of five keystroke combinations that will pop most kiosks, but we'll only mention one—a combo that doesn't get mentioned much. A good friend of mine, CP, has this wild ability to make machines do crazy things, as these next photos reveal. CP took this next photo of an employment kiosk in its natural environment.

The designers of this particular machine were pretty smart—they removed most of the keys that evil hackers (script kiddies) use to mess the thing up. Even still, the *SHIFT* key is there and CP puts it to good use. He taps it five times, and the kiosk springs to life with an annoying chirp, thanks to the Windows *sticky keys* function. The popup in the next photo signals the beginning of the fun.

The *sticky keys* popup snaps the kiosk out of kiosk mode and into Windows mode. This gives CP access to the *Start* menu and the taskbar, visible in the next photo.

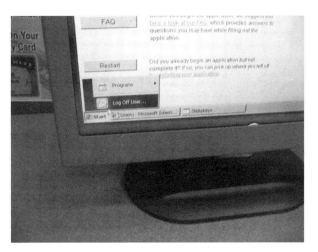

Although the Windows session is still very limited, the taskbar reveals an awful lot. We can see that the kiosk program is called *Unicru* (www.kronos.com), and a Google search shows that it is human resource application software run by the likes of Lowe's, Hollywood Video, Circuit City, Toys R Us, Best Buy, Whole Foods and Blockbuster Video. This is interesting because it suggests that this sticky keys "attack" will work against their application kiosks as well. The next photo shows the right-hand side of the task bar.

This photo reveals that the kiosks run VNC servers on addresses owned by the Department of Defense Network Information Center. I'm not sure exactly what that means. But CP just might have discovered that major retail chains are actually under the control of the United States Department of Defense. That explains the drill-sergeant attitude of some of the cashiers.

CP has poked at other kiosks as well. This next photo shows a custom kiosk used by a national bookstore chain. Unlike the hospital kiosks, this was put in the store intentionally for customers to interact with. During slow hours, a low-tech hacker could goof around for many minutes without arousing suspicion.

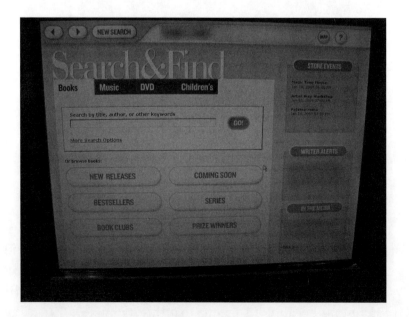

A few whacks of the *SHIFT* key produces the sticky keys configuration, along with other accessibility options as shown in the next photo.

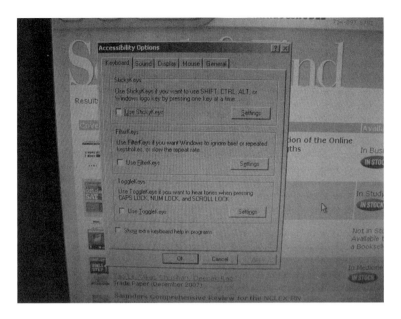

The sticky keys "hack" won't work against every kiosk, but it works against quite a few of them, and it's another shining example of a simple no-tech hack that can sidestep modern security restrictions.

Real World: ATM Hacking

E-ticket terminals, employment kiosks, medical records kiosks and the like are interesting, but the undisputed king of the kiosk is the Automated Teller Machine (ATM). I mean come on—the thing holds *cash*. It's a natural target for all sorts of attackers, the high-tech and no-tech alike. When I saw the scene in the next photo, I had to grab a shot.

The two technicians were so into their work that they hardly noticed me. I snapped a few more photos, and eventually the tech in the blue shirt got a call on his cell phone and wandered off. Although he remained close to his post, I knew he was multitasking and he would be oblivious to the world around him. I took the opportunity to move in closer. I stood next to the machine, just out of view of the laptop jockey on the other side. I looked down and snapped the next photo.

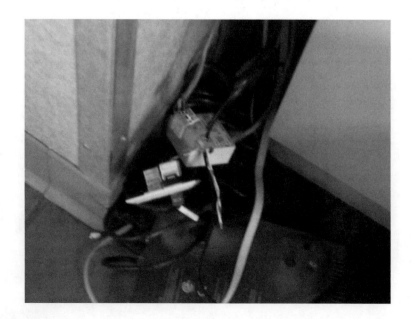

The mess of wires was interesting. I recognized them as standard network cables. I recognized the gray device at the bottom of the photo and snapped a better photo of it.

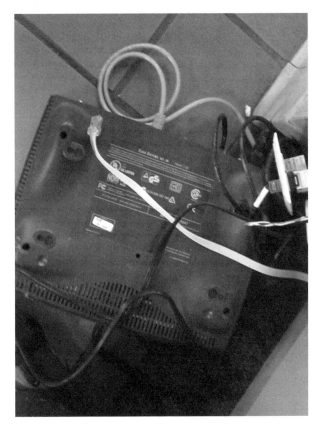

The Cisco 1700 series router looked decidedly old, but at least it was recognizable. I hadn't done much research into ATM machines, but I had always thought of them as really oddball machines that relied on weird hardware and proprietary protocols. The network cables suggested that a common protocol (like TCP/IP) was in use, and the Cisco router reinforced this. Looking behind the ATM, I saw the network wire trailing from the back of the machine and wondered if it always stuck out from the machine. That also made me wonder if I could come back later and attach my own hub or router and fiddle with the machine. As the blue-shirt finished up his phone call and returned to his post, I backed away from the machine. I knew I'd never come back to try out my theories about the network cables. I knew where that road led, and I had no intention of getting locked up for my curiosity. I walked across the hall, keeping my eye on the techs. Blue-shirt opened up the front of the cabinet, and his cell phone rang again. He walked away, and I got a great shot of the ATM's innards.

Tucked inside the machine was what looked like a standard PC desktop, lying on its side. I knew that I could probably get more information by Googling the name of the ATM machine and digging up the manual (yes, that works) but this was more fun. I was a visitor in the building (did I mention that I was scheduled to give a talk on No-Tech Hacking?) and despite a constant stream of traffic and my distinct lack of a visitor's badge, here I was lurking around taking photos of the ATM techs. Googling just wouldn't have been the same. I snapped a picture of blue-shirt's laptop, all alone on the top of the machine.

I can't talk too much about what I saw on that screen, or what that little antenna-looking thing was on the side of his computer or what the ATM technician used it for, because that would be irresponsible. I also can neither confirm nor deny any information I may have about how (or if) the technician interacted with the safe inside the machine and whether or not he may (or may not have) been susceptible to shoulder surfing as he fiddled (or did not fiddle) with the safe. Besides, my target was the other guy—he looked like the real techie. I swung to my right, stood behind him, and snapped a photo.

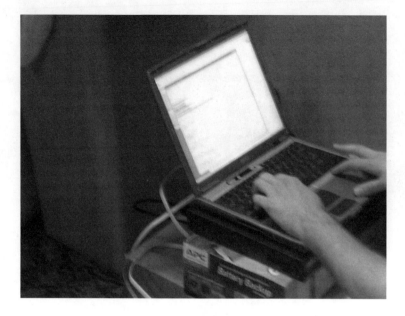

I (could have) captured video, too, and (might have) become very familiar with the tools, protocols and processes he used (or may not have used) to interact with the ATM machine. If I were a bad guy, I might have been well on my way to pulling off my first ATM heist, thanks to a good no-tech hacking session. And no, I never returned to that ATM. Nor do I plan to.

Chapter 10

Vehicle Surveillance

No spy movie is complete without a car chase scene. But that requires lots of takes, slick editing and a monster budget, all to create something thrilling, but fake. What most people don't realize that some of the most thrilling vehicular espionage happens when the cars aren't moving at all?

How Easy Is Vehicle Surveillance?

Whether I'm on my way into a client building I intend to break into, or just strolling around, I notice vehicles. I'm not like a car nut who enjoys interesting, old, or exotic cars, but I get a certain (odd) thrill out of building a profile of the driver by looking at their car. No-tech hackers are really good at this, and in this chapter, I'll give you an idea of what they look for. Check out the next photo. What can you tell me about the driver?

Ok, I'll admit—we're starting easy. Besides the bristling antennas poking out of every panel and window, there's a metal plate (shown below) that spells out exactly what kind of vehicle this is, and what line of work the driver's in.

If you guessed that the car was an "undercover" or "unmarked" police car, you're right, and you might just have a knack for vehicle surveillance. Taking the next logic jump, it's safe to assume the driver's either a police officer or he just jacked an officer's ride.

Let's take a look at another one. What can you tell me about the driver of the vehicle shown in the next photo?

The tag reads "U.S. Government" and "For Official Use Only." If you guessed *government employee*, congratulations—you're on a real tear. Keep it up. Let's look at another example. Check out the next photo. It's more obvious what the driver of this vehicle *does* for a living, but what would a no-tech hacker consider doing with this information?

When I first saw this van, I thought *social engineering*. With the right shirt, sporting the right logo, I could be the "Acme" Bank Security & Vault Services guy, ready to work on this company's safes, vaults, pneumatic systems or alarm systems (not that a hacker would be at all interested in those things). Let's try another exercise. Take a look at the next photo.

Most normal people would just see a crowded parking lot. A soccer mom would know right away that this was the parking lot of a Kohl's department store and they would hang an immediate left, drawn in by the "biggest sale of the season" which just so happens to run every other week. A book weenie (like me) would recognize the Barnes and Noble bookstore across the parking lot. A no-tech hacker would immediately think "fed"—slang for *federal agent*, a term used to identify federal government employees. How would he realize this? Can you tell from the above photo? If you can't quite tell, take a look at the next photo, which highlights the "fed's" vehicle.

Stepping closer, a no-tech hacker would realize that the dark car was indeed owned by a government employee, and he or she would also know approximately where that employee reported for work. All of this information and more can be gleaned from the vehicle permit stuck on the window, like the one shown below.

These stickers are everywhere, especially in areas that maintain a large military or government presence, such as military bases and government-owned business corridors. Many installations also use color-coded permits, like the ones shown in the next photo.

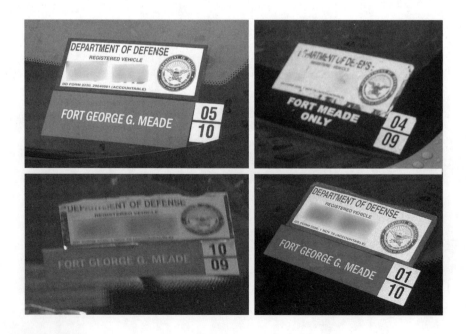

The colors (or shades of gray, thanks to the spectrally challenged nature of black and white printing) of these permits are significant, as they reveal the employee's status and/or rank. In some cases, the rank is more predominantly displayed, as the next photo shows.

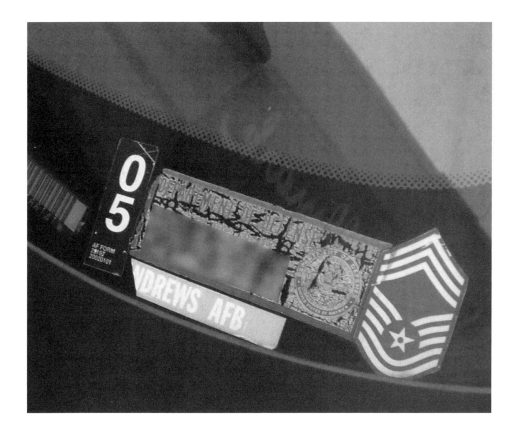

In this particular case, a quick Google search reveals that the owner of the vehicle is Chief Master Sergeant in the U.S. Air Force.

Some stickers just make me chuckle, like the one below.

It's not so much the sticker that's funny, it's that acronym—IHDIVNAVSURFWAR CEN. That's got to be one of the longest acronyms I've ever seen in real life. I was tempted to follow this car so I could find out exactly what a "surf war" looked like. It would certainly give new meaning to "shooting the curl." Government employees aren't the only ones eyeballed by no-tech hackers. A quick glance at the Volvo in the next photo reveals either where the owner works or lives. Can you tell how?

The answer lies not in the license plate or VIN number of the vehicle, but rather in the window sticker, shown below.

Photo courtesy Garland Glessner

Oil change stickers like this one seem pretty innocuous, but a no-tech hacker can use simple deduction to realize that the address is probably close to where the owner works or lives. If the vehicle is parked in a work parking lot, and the address isn't local, it probably is near their home. Most people won't get an oil change somewhere that's out of the way of their normal commute.

In some cases, it's easy to get a history of a driver by looking at their vehicle. Judging from the next photo, can you tell me what city the driver lives in, what part of that city, and approximately how long they have lived there?

Photo courtesy Garland Glessner

The city is easy to figure out—it's spelled out on the parking permit. Guessing how long he or she has lived in San Francisco is pretty straightforward, considering the first parking permit expired in July of 2000. Figuring out where the driver lives in San Francisco take a bit of creativity. However, Google is a no-tech hacker's friend. A quick search for *San Francisco residential parking permit map* leads us to a handy PDF map, a portion of which is shown below.

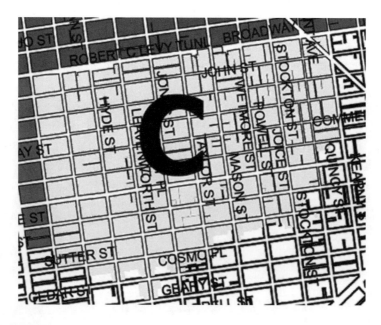

The map clearly labels where, exactly, the permit is valid, pointing us to the approximate area where the driver lives. The next photo is quite similar, and can be used to deduce the same information, but in this case, a no-tech hacker can also determine where the driver lived previously and when they moved. Can you?

Photo courtesy Garland Glessner

Judging from the dates on the parking permits, the driver moved from San Francisco residential permit area *"A"* to residential permit area *"C"* sometime between February and June of 2004. Using the map we Googled above, we can get a good idea of exactly where both residential permit areas are in San Francisco.

So far we've only looked at the exterior of the vehicle. Although there are many other things we could use to deduce information using only exterior clues, some of the best stuff is often sitting inside a vehicle in plain site of anyone passing by--like the receipt in the next photo. Although I had to fiddle with the zoom on my crappy camera to capture the document instead of the raindrops on the window, I think the photo came out quite nicely.

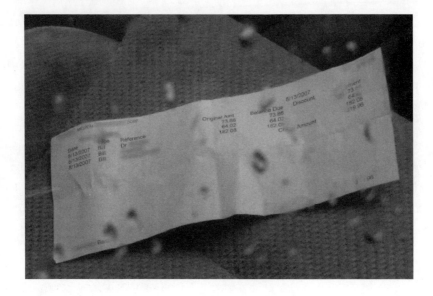

This receipt lists a doctor's name, address and phone number, the patient's (presumably the driver's) name and insurance company, a list of services performed on that particular date, and what the charges were for those services. Most people guard their medical information very closely, but I'm constantly surprised by how often I see information like this out in the open.

The one thing more important than medical data to most people (and most identity thieves) is financial data. I captured this photo in an employee parking lot. The document belongs to a senior level executive.

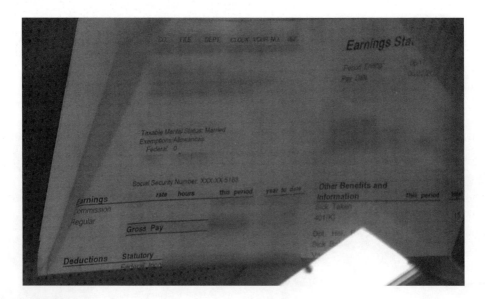

As you can see, it reveals the employee's name, benefit information, net and gross pay, tax information and more. The most valuable piece of information, in my opinion, is the revelation of the last four digits of the employee's social security number, which is used as a security question by most automated identity verification systems. Armed with this information, I could easily establish credit in this person's name or steal their identity completely.

Of course, I tend to get all worked up when I catch information like this out in the open, but as the next photo reminds me, some people just don't care about protecting their privacy. That is exactly why identity theft will continue to be a thriving criminal business.

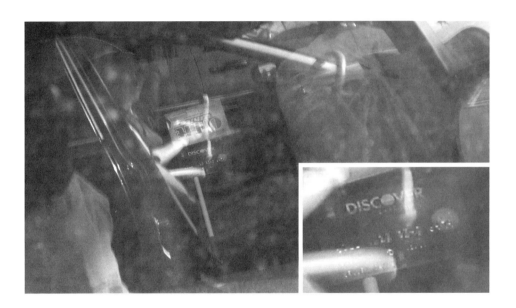

I can't resist, so here goes the bad pun—"It pays to Discover." The digits from this credit card could easily be used to make purchases from any vendor that doesn't abide by rather strict credit card screening procedures, and many of them do not. If you've got your medical records, bank statement or credit cards sitting on your front seat, there's a good chance a no-tech hacker will have seen it before you get around to removing it. As I've said in other chapters, the key to protecting yourself is to remain vigilant, and try to see life through the eyes of a no-tech hacker. Check out the Epilogue for more good advice.

Chapter 11

Badge Surveillance

Where Are Your Badges?

I like slipping into buildings as the phone guy. It's my favorite getup, because I've got the gear, the lingo, and the outfit. But without the official-looking badge, I'm just some nimrod with a bag of gadgets and a dorky shirt. The badge makes the look, and the look makes me the phone guy. But isn't a badge nothing more than a laminated bit of paper? No, it's really so much more than that. In security lingo, it's an *authentication token*. When I present it to someone, they look at it and draw a conclusion about who I am. Visual identification makes for weak authentication, but that's how it works inside most of my target buildings, so I leverage that fatal security flaw. Knowing that a no-tech hacker can easily duplicate a badge after sneaking one quick look, I'm pretty surprised at the hundreds of badges I spot out in the open every single week.

Even though I catch these silly things out in the open so often, I still get giddy when I see a new one because I know beyond a shadow of a doubt that I could somehow use it to gain access to that company. Even if they employ some sort of electronic system to validate the card—we'll talk more about those systems later in this chapter—I could probably use the badge to tailgate or social engineer my way inside. Getting giddy about site badges is weird, I know, but I've come to accept that I'm just not normal. So these days I go all the way. I carry a camera wherever I go to capture badges I spot in the wild, like the one in the next photo which I spotted flapping around in a local mall.

Many times, badges appear in packs, as the next photo reveals.

As I waited in the lobby of a large corporate building (on legitimate business of course) I was sucked into the drone of a corporate cheerleading slideshow spewing from the wall-mounted flat screen. Right before I lapsed into a fit of bored unconsciousness, I saw the screen shown in the next photo. I nearly fell over in my armchair trying to get my camera out in time.

This slide was one of several that showed groups of employees—in various stages of corporate bonding—all wearing their badges. I had no real interest in popping this building, but after two minutes in the lobby, I had more than enough info to forge a laminated paper access token, and attempt to have my way with the building.

Government agencies have known for years that employee badges should be removed when leaving the workplace. The more secretive agencies are very proactive when it comes to enforcing this policy. I was not surprised to discover so few open-air badges around more secretive government buildings. The keyword here is *few*. While spending some time in the D.C. corridor, I came upon an outdoor barbeque catered by an office leasing company. The event was designed to show appreciation for the various corporate tenants, some of which were government related. As I wandered around the large catering tent, I was amazed at the number of badges I spotted. I was so busy snapping pictures of people that I nearly forgot to chow down on the free grub.

Although I saw badges belonging to several different companies, some were more surprising than others, such as the airfield badge here.

I'm pretty sure I can't just waltz onto the airfield with a flimsy look–alike badge, but the photo is interesting nonetheless considering it was taken well away from airport property. At this point, I will refuse to mention the recent spate of news stories about the TSA misplacing several hundred uniforms. I can also neither confirm nor deny whether it is or is not possible to gain unauthorized access to any airport property when decked out in (or not decked out in) a TSA uniform.

As I continued to mill around the catering tent, two women waiting in line caught my eye (not in that way). The taller of the two was very important-looking. She was dressed in a smart black suit and was having an important-sounding conversation on her Blackberry. It wasn't the geek-chic cell phone that caught my eye, but rather the plethora of badges and paraphernalia dangling from her lanyard. Traveling in tech circles, I've seen my share of lanyard clutter, but this lady took the prize for most neck-flair toted by a female.

As I drew closer, I realized that her badge was decidedly government-ish. I took a few photos—which neither of them seemed to notice—and after checking them out I realized I had a horrible angle on the more interesting badge. As she continued chatting into the phone, I swung around to the other side of her and stepped in as close as I could without triggering her (admittedly impaired) stalker detection system. Less than a foot away from her, I snapped the next photo.

This particular badge is issued to government employees stationed at the Pentagon. The Post-It note reminds her to "bring a copy of yesterday's all hands to DSS H.Q."

Granted, security at the Pentagon is second to none. I know from personal experience that the guards stationed at the Pentagon mean business. They are not to be trifled with. I also know that visual identification of a badge at the Pentagon means absolutely nothing. All badges are electronically verified, and the security of that electronic process is world-class. I'm also pretty sure those wicked-looking automatic rifles the guards have are real.

Still, I think the Pentagon security squad would flip if they knew how casual their employees were with their badges. I'm not pointing my finger at the Pentagon, but I think it's important to mention that even the most die-hard government agencies hire sometimes-careless human beings. The *policies* in place at the Pentagon ensure that careless behavior does not negatively impact the security posture of the facility, and corporate security officers should take this lesson to heart. Visual identification of an employee badge is not a secure authentication mechanism. Do not allow any avenue for social engineers. Establish a secure access mechanism and back it up with sound, enforceable policy that employees understand and are bound to. Employees should understand that security is not someone else's problem.

Electronic Badge Authentication

I think I have successfully established that visual badge identification is an insecure security procedure. Electronic verification is a much more secure method of authentication, but these systems have security issues as well and the no-tech attacks against them are pretty interesting. It's not uncommon to see proximity-type cards in plain view, as the next photo shows.

High-Tech Badge Attacks

Many technological differences exist between *swipe* cards and *proximity* or *contactless* cards, but they can be attacked in similar ways. Both can be copied, but thanks to the device developed by Jonathan Westhues (detailed at http://cq.cx/prox.pl) contactless cards can be copied from a distance even when they are carried in a pocket or purse. To prevent this type of attack, consider combining access cards with PIN identification schemes, or deploy a system that relies on encryption, challenge-response systems, or reader access lists, like HiD's *iClass* line.

This pair had executed good common sense and removed their site badges. However, their access cards were still in plain view. Although the possibility existed for cloning the cards, in the spirit of no-tech hacking, an alternative attack is possible. An adversary can simply look at the card to learn a lot about it. Consider the typical *Datawatch* card shown in the next photo.

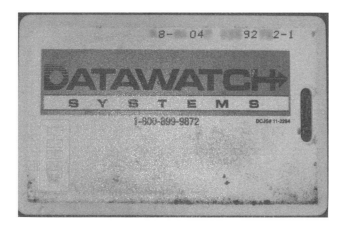

The toll-free number on the card rings through to Datawatch Systems. All an adversary has to do is call the number speak to (or mildly social engineer) a representative, read off the top row of numbers, and learn not only the address and building number the card will work on, but in some cases the suite or room number as well.

Most people would never consider wearing a Post-It note on their forehead revealing their work address, but it's surprising how many people wear these electronic cards in plain sight which reveal essentially the same stuff. Access cards like these should be removed when leaving a work area.

Real World Badge Surveillance

CP sends me this great story of a beautiful social engineering of his phone repairman's badge. CP's style made the story even funnier, so I've included it in his own words.

"A [telco] employee came into my work to fix our DSL2 line, while he was working I tripped him up on some [telco] policy and insinuated that he may not actually be from [the telco] (someone no tech hacking me) and that I needed pictures of his badge as a "security reference". He then asked me why I needed this and I told him it was just a personal policy and that he really didn't need to comply, and yet he handed me his badge lanyard and continued to work while I took pictures of his [three company] badges. He seemed a little nervous while I was taking the pictures with my cell phone camera, but afterwards I offered him a Sprite and a shot of Patrón which we had sitting in the office. He declined the booze but took the soda. That seemed to loosen him up a bit." -CP

The next three (highly edited photos) are proof of CP's success.

Photos courtesy CP

The attack was purposefully simple, but incredibly elegant. By calling his curiosity a "personal policy" and offering the technician an easy out, he made himself seem less threatening (CP is one of the good guys after all). By offering the guy a drink, he put the tech's mind at ease, and it's very likely that he never reported the incident. Had CP been one of the bad guys, there could easily be a no-tech telco "repairman" in your offices right now.

This next real-world hack combines a couple of techniques into one successful attack. As I was driving around one day, I spotted a very distinct government blue-badger out for a lunchtime stroll. Since I was driving through a normal-looking office park, the appearance of a govie badge surprised me. By the time I turned my car around to get a photo, I lost track of the govie. I pulled into one of the many parking lots and drove around to try to figure out which building belonged to the government. All of the buildings looked the same, and many of them were unmarked, which made my job even more difficult. I thought of glancing inside some of the dumpsters, but since this wasn't a pay gig, I thought better of it—gigs can go bad quickly without a *get out of jail free* card. Instead, I continued to cruise the parking lots in search of more badges. Then I spotted a familiar parking permit. I walked up to the vehicle and snapped the next photo.

As I looked around the lot, I realized that every other vehicle around one particular building sported a DoD parking permit. I knew beyond any shadow of a doubt that I had found the government building. I hopped back in my car and started doing slow laps around the building, watching for employees. After a few laps, I saw the guy in the next picture come out of the building. Do you see what I saw?

The blue badge was perfectly clear in the unaltered image, and I recognized it immediately as belonging to a very interesting Government agency. The guy in the photo looked right at me as I drove past filming him out the window, but he didn't seem to notice. He was busy chatting on his cell phone. I decided to park my car and walk around the building on foot. I walked past several employees as I lapped the building, and found it difficult to discreetly capture badge photos while walking, so I gave up on discretion and just started filming like a normal person. With the camera up to eye level, I captured the next still as a video clip.

If the woman in the photo noticed me, she didn't say anything to me. I didn't acknowledge her either—I was busy with my camera. Next, I decided to camp outside one of the side entrances. I put my camera on a curb with the lens facing the door, and let it film. I stood next to the camera, and every now and then I would bend down and fiddle with the laces on my shoes (I hadn't worn my special Velcro sneakers that day). This, of course made me seem less like a suspicious camper. I caught lots of great stills, like the one shown below.

Although it must have looked odd to see me standing there on the curb, no one asked any questions, so I remained a while longer. This camping trip resulted in the shot I used in the tailgating section, which began with the employee in the next photo entering the building.

Ten seconds after she passed through the door, it was only closed about halfway.

The door took a full fifteen seconds to close, making it one of the slowest-closing doors I had ever personally witnessed. This of course would provide a bad guy plenty of time to make it through unnoticed. Although I use this government facility as an example, I've seen hundreds of corporate buildings that have even more lax security than this. The point here is that despite the advent of advanced security systems, most of them rely on *people*, who are often lazy, uninformed or both. No-tech hackers realize this, and will prey on this security weakness in creative and often effective ways.

All through this book you've seen examples where people noticed me not only spying on them, but recording them and their environments. Why didn't they stop me or alert someone? Perhaps some of them didn't care. But in most cases, people don't react because they don't know what to do. If you want the folks in your organization to challenge trespassers or report odd incidents, you need to do two things well:

1) Provide incentives for reporting suspicious activities. This doesn't have to mean money. Recognition and praise at company gatherings sends the signal that "alert = good" and proactive people will be rewarded.

2) Make your desired response both well known and easy to do.

Honestly…if you saw me outside your office zooming in on your PC and snapping pictures, do you know who you should notify? Do your co-workers? It's not enough to have an "Intrusion Response Policy" if no one knows what it is. Publicize it periodically and repeatedly, rehearse it, and who knows–maybe in the next few months, you'll bag yourself a few no-tech hackers!

Top Ten Ways to Shut Down No-Tech Hackers

If you're responsible for defending against the bad guy versions of no-tech hackers like me, you'll need to develop some of the same awareness. A no-tech hacker will spot that sensitive document laying out in public, unless you spot it first. A no-tech hacker will notice the ineffective lock on the "To Be Shredded" bin, unless you notice it first. Even though you never heard a whistle blow, the game is already in progress. Are you ready to match wits with a malicious, highly motivated foe? If not, read on - and get off the bench, before it's "Game Over."

Now that we're clear on what the bad guys can accomplish, let's review what can be done to keep them at bay. Presented in no particular order, here are the ten best ways to shut down no-tech hackers.

Go Undercover

Keep it Secret. Gandalf had it right when he said, "Keep it secret, keep it safe." Don't work on private stuff in public spaces, and don't make yourself a target. Be aware of the profile you present, and tone it down if necessary. If you've got to work on private stuff in public, consider a laptop privacy filter. Of course bear in mind that an experienced shoulder surfer will see a privacy filter and rightly assume you're working on something sensitive. Because of this, the mere existence of a filter can make you or your machine a target. Did I mention leaving the private stuff out of public spaces? That's your best bet.

Play it smart. You might be proud of the company you work for, but sometimes flying the team colors is a bad idea. Depending on current events, the political climate or other factors anyone can become a target of public scrutiny or unwanted attention. Government agencies have requested for years that employees travel low profile, but those same agencies still produce signature items sporting the agency logo. The best advice I can offer you is to play it smart. Take a moment to consider your profile, and every now and then play it paranoid. A no-tech hacker may be the least of your worries.

Say no to Stickers. If you're forced to have company stickers on your gear, consider putting a sticky note over them when you're traveling. This will at least keep the sticker (and the information that can be inferred from it) hidden from too-curious eyes.

Let's (not) Go To Lunch. Jack Wiles reminds us that it's all too easy to have private conversations in public spaces, especially when grabbing a bite with coworkers. Be aware that no-tech hackers love to hang out at the corporate watering hole or food trough. So, don't fill their all-too-eager ears with company jargon and secrets.

Shred Everything

The golden rule is to shred everything. But shredding is a subjective word. There are lots of varieties of shredders, each of which provides a different level of security. While a basic shredder that churns out 3/8" strip seems decent enough, it's trivial to reassemble the pieces. Obliterating your docs with a particle shredder is nice, but those things are pretty expensive, and unless you're truly evil (or paranoid), it's just overkill.

A decent "micro-cut" shredder from an office supply store will cost around $200, and can cut paper, CD's and even credit cards into 3/32 x 5/16 pieces, for better than average security. Generally speaking, you'll get what you pay for. But whatever you choose anything's better that putting documents in the trash in one piece, or laying them in the parking lot.

It's also a great idea to get to know what's in your trash before the bad guys do. If you're in charge of security for your company, consider at least a weekly visit to your dumpster to get a feel for what's being tossed and what condition it's in when it lands in the big green box. If you're a consumer looking to protect your privacy, get a personal shredder and have a discussion with your family members about what should be shredded before being thrown away. If your family refuses to comply, you might consider relocating them.

Get Decent Locks

Forget everything you've seen on TV—all locks are not created equal. Our experts chime in on selecting a good lock. We've already seen that many locks can be shimmed. Deviant Ollam says we can shutdown shimmers by selecting shim-proof locks. Here's his advice for selecting a shim-proof lock:

- Select a lock that can only be shut by using the key or combination.

- Select a *key retaining padlock*, which hangs onto the key when the lock is open.

- Look for "double ball" mechanism locks.

- Select padlocks which feature a *collar* or *boot* on the shackle.

This is great advice, but I found myself asking the obvious question: "Which locks do the pros recommend?" Deviant Ollam and Marc Tobias offered solid, immediate responses:

- EVVA MCS (www.evva.at/at/technology/mcs): Given the choice of one lock, both experts agree: "Give me the MCS padlock."

- Schlage Everest Primus (http://everestprimus.schlage.com): Deviant and Marc both agree: the Primus is excellent. Deviant says, "They were making a wickedly pick-resistant and totally bump-proof lock before the media had ever even caught on to the problem."

- Abloy Protec (www.abloy.com.au): Deviant says, "The company is great about refining their design to make many attacks ineffective."

- Sargent & Greenleaf 8088 and 8077 series locks (http://www.sargentandgreenleaf. com): These puppies are often found on Department of Defense filing cabinets.

Jack Wiles also weighs in, saying that the ABUS Diskus (http://www.acelock.com), which he recommends as an "odd-shaped, but all around decent" standby.

Also, keep in mind that no matter how secure your locking systems may be, you should always keep your keys out of sight of the bad guys. Barry Wels of The Open Organization of Lockpickers (Toool) reminds us that professionals can "read" a key just by looking at it, giving him a head start on either duplicating the key or picking the lock it was made for. He even reports to have heard rumors that "surveillance teams try to make photographs of keys visibly worn by suspects to give the NDE (non-destructive operator) a head start ...." He goes on to say in his blog at www.toool.nl/blackbag that some prison guards "carry keys in a way the inmates can not see them." One solution is to consider a customized key carrying device like a "key port" from www.key-port. com, which conceals the keys from view, but makes them simple to take out when they are needed.

Jack Wiles also suggests some sound physical security advice:

- Check all locks at work and home, and report or fix any that are malfunctioning.

- Don't prop doors open, and report any that you do find propped open.

- Get all your locks re-keyed when you move into any home, and when you suspect that someone has been inside.

- Always consult a professional to evaluate the physical security of your home or workplace.

Put that Badge Away

Like Doris "Mama Soul" Troy used to sing, "Just one look, that's all it took, yeah just one look." This oldie's hook is like a no-tech hacker's anthem. One look is all a no-tech hacker needs to memorize, duplicate, laminate, infiltrate and frustrate. Put that badge away. It really is that simple.

Check Your Surveillance Gear

If you can bypass your own security cameras and motion sensors, a bad guy can too (and probably already has). Test out all your surveillance gear, and consider the following advice:

- Better quality cameras are less susceptible to bright light attacks.

- Domes and films can deter flaring attacks, but remember that any optic treatment can block light the camera relies on, like the infrared light used by low-light cameras.

- Use multiple cameras with fully overlapping views.

- Consider armored housing and protect the camera's video feed and power source from physical attack.

- Hidden cameras never hurt, especially when mixed with more obvious units.

Shut Down Shoulder Surfers

Watch your angles. Remain aware of the angles that shoulder surfers rely on. Don't put yourself in situations that invite shoulder surfers. Position your back to the wall when using your machine, and never leave it unattended. Don't wear company logos and remove extraneous markings and information from your mobile computing devices, especially if your company name might entice an adversary. The tech support folks in your shop can probably provide you a long list of tech things to avoid when traveling. Follow their advice.

Keep those digits to yourself. What's the point of any kind of pass code if you enter it in plain site of everyone? When entering sensitive data, create some sort of barrier between the keys and wandering eyes. This might require you to reposition your body, or create a shield with your spare hand. If you aren't willing to do this, why have a pass code at all?

Throw down! I'm not suggesting you body tackle every oddball that might be shoulder surfing you. What I would suggest is that you close your laptop (or turn off your monitor) if you think you're a target and become suddenly (and obviously) interested in something else, like sipping your coffee. Most no-tech hackers will know they've been busted and move along. If they do bail, keep a casual eye on them as they leave and try to get a good look at them and their car/bike/skateboard/Segway before they bail. When they've cleared out take a look at what you were working on, consider all of it compromised, and act accordingly. If your surfer doesn't bail after you close your lid, keep an eye on him or her anyhow. If he or she continues acting suspiciously, do something about it. Inform a manager, security guard or hall monitor. Do *something*. If that something involves physical violence, just don't tell the judge it was my idea.

Block Tailgaters

Don't let them in. If someone you don't recognize attempts to tailgate behind you, slam the door on their wanna-be hacker fingers. That will not only keep them out of your building, but will also put a serious cramp in their Google-hacking mojo. If they turn out not to be a hacker, apologize and take them out for lunch. Be nice and make it a place with some one-handed fare—fast food joints offer a great selection. Strangers will come to fear you, but the security goons will love you, and that's important.

Err on the side of caution. Don't settle for taking the world at face value. Too many people see a logo or a uniform and make bad assumptions. Don't be that person. If your Spidey-sense tells you something's wrong, it probably is. If you don't have Spidey-sense, walk loudly and carry a big stick. Whatever you do, don't let the security of your home or workplace rest on poor assumptions.

Quit Smoking. I love smoking entrances. They are my preferred method of entry to even the most secured facilities. So either quit smoking, buck the system and just smoke in the office, or remember that the stranger hanging outside with you might just be me.

Policy rhymes with "juicy," kind of. Policies are good. As Jack Wiles shares, "Unless there is a strong corporate policy requiring all employees to challenge anyone that they can't identify, [tailgating] is a difficult problem to deal with. At an absolute minimum, employees should be trained on when and how to notify security if they suspect that an unauthorized person has followed them in."

Clean your Car

Stickers are not your friends. No-tech hackers can tell an *awful* lot by checking out your car's stickers. If you don't absolutely need them, take them off. The worst offenders are oil change stickers, parking permits and membership stickers. Some required stickers don't need to be permanently attached. If you can get away with it, mount the sticker to an index card, and store it behind your visor when you aren't using it.

Get rid of that junk. Remember the old adage of the eight P's: "Printouts, paychecks, personal and private papers persuade peeping people." So it's not exactly wisdom of the ages, but I guess it works. That junk in your car might be much more than an eyesore—it might provide information that a bad guy could use to profile you. Prevent profiling by practicing proper pick-up. And avoid a pithy saying battle when your opponent is armed with a thesaurus.

Play it smart, G-Man. Government parking permits on cars in the parking lot indicate a government facility is nearby. Be extra vigilant if you work in a building that contains a large number of these permits, and be on your guard as the building may be the target of an attack in the form of a tailgating, social engineering, dumpster diving exercise—or worse.

Watch your Back Online

Avoid Instant Messaging profile pitfalls. We could do an entire book on the privacy implications of using instant messenger (IM) programs. When you sign up for a new IM user account, most services create all sorts of personal data trails that a hacker or identity thief could uncover. Never enter personal information about yourself that you wouldn't give to a personal stranger. Also, make sure your client is set to confirm every action a remote user might take such as uploads, downloads and requests for profile information. Poorly configured IM clients are bad news if you're concerned about your privacy.

Keep an eye on P2P software. It's scary to think about a hacker targeting your personal information, but understand that P2P hacking is not about targeting specific individuals. P2P hacking is about finding interesting information based on specific keywords. If a hacker's after you, he or she is probably not going to log into a P2P client in search of your information because this makes the assumption that you're running a P2P client *and* that you have shared personal data there. Both of these are rather wild assumptions. So if you do run P2P software, make sure you know exactly what it is you are sharing, and then make sure your personal firewall, and virus/ spyware/adware software is current and correctly configured.

Google yourself. Even if it's not your fault, your personal information can end up landing on the Web. If it gets on the Web, Google will crawl it. If Google crawls it, your stuff's open to the low-tech hacking techniques of Google hackers. Googling yourself is never a bad idea, but remember that Googling an entire credit card number or all the digits of your social security number is a bad idea—the search term itself then becomes private data. Instead, search for your name and address, or a portion of your name along with a portion of a sensitive number. Better yet, use the *numrange* operator to search for your name along with a range of numbers *around* those sensitive digits. For more on advanced searching with Google, I've heard that *Google Hacking for Penetration Testers* from Syngress publishing is pretty decent.

Beware of Social Engineers

It's not about the giving. For a social engineer, it's about getting something. You might not know when you're being conned, but whenever a stranger elicits sensitive information from you, it's a distinct possibility.

Stay constantly aware. "Every unknown voice on the phone is a potential Social Engineer," says Jack Wiles, "until I feel otherwise. I'm not paranoid, just careful."

Get into a program. If you're in charge of security for your company, Jack suggests you conduct social engineering awareness training explaining how to avoid becoming a victim. He goes on to say that security awareness training is the overall least expensive and most effective countermeasure that you can employ in your security plan. He also suggests role playing as a way of showing what social engineering looks like, and social engineering "tiger team" attacks that focus on uncovering and revealing weaknesses and sharing lessons learned with employees.

Index